Fabulous
Lo-Carb
Cuisine

Ruth Glick

Light Street Press
Columbia, Maryland

FABULOUS LO-CARB CUISINE
Ruth Glick

Copyright © 2001 by Ruth Glick

Light Street Press
P. O. Box 1233
Columbia, MD 21044-0233

Cover Design by Sanny Wroblewski

Library of Congress Catalog Card Number: 00-193116

Glick, Ruth B.
  Fabulous Lo-Carb Cuisine / Ruth Glick
    p. cm.
  ISBN 0-9706293-0-3
  1. Cookery. 2. Low-carbohydrate diet--Recipes. I. Title
  641.5 2001

ISBN: 0-9706293-0-3

+
0 9 8 7 6 5 4 3 2

Printed in the United States of America

CONTENTS

Asian Steak
Beef Paprikash
Tangy Pot Roast with Vegetables
Barbecued Beef Brisket
Sweet and Sour Ground Beef and Cabbage
Greek Lasagna
Stuffed Peppers, Greek-Style
Lasagna Peppers
Mexican Stuffed Peppers
Philly Cheese Steak
Sloppy Joes
Barbecued Spare Ribs
Pork Chops with Sauerkraut and Tomato
Italian Chicken with Peppers and Onions
Greek-Style Chicken
Kung Pao Chicken
Orange Roughy, Mediterranean-Style
Grilled Fresh Salmon with Dill
Shrimp with Olives and Feta Cheese
Creamy Tuna over Broccoli
Salmon Pie
Bacon and Cheese Omelet
Broccoli-Cheese Omelet
Pan Pizza Omelet
Ham and Onion Quiche
Broccoli-Cheddar Quiche
Southwestern Quiche
Salmon Quiche

Peanut Cookies
Toffee-Flavored Pecans
Pecan Crust
Marzipan Crust
Fruit Pizza
Key Lime Pie
Mocha Pie
Cheesecake
Lemon Mousse
Strawberry Mousse
Vanilla Ice Cream
Strawberry Ice Cream
Coffee Ice Cream
Frozen Strawberry Cream Pie
Sweetened Whipped Cream
Pecan Cake
Creme Anglaise
Tart Shells
Strawberry Tarts
Strawberry Whipped Cream Tarts
Pecan Custard Tarts
Pecan Cream Cheese Tarts
Hot Mocha

HELPFUL LO-CARB PRODUCTS

ACKNOWLEDGMENTS

An enormous amount of testing went into the recipes for *Fabulous Lo-Carb Cuisine*. I could never have accomplished all the tests and retests without Bill Spinelli and Martin Mendelson who cooked many of the recipes in my kitchen and offered suggestions on techniques as well as for improvement in appearance, taste appeal, and flavor. Linda Yoakam, who did the nutritional analysis on each recipe, helped me lower the carb content on dishes that were too high. And Sanny Wroblewski who designed the fabulous cover.

I also want to thank my friends and family, especially my husband Norman Glick who persuaded me to write this book and who did the typesetting and proofreading. Marilyn Wankum, who first urged us to try lo-carb cooking. Mary Kilchenstein, who exchanged recipe ideas and techniques with me. My Thursday writing group and Elissa and Steve Webber who tasted many of these dishes in their various versions and made many helpful comments. And Eliot and Brenda Sohmer, who also cheered me on.

CONFESSIONS OF A LO-CARB COOK

I've had a love affair with cooking since I was tall enough to reach the controls on the stove. There's nothing more satisfying to me than putting together a mouthwatering combination of flavors--then watching family and friends enjoy my culinary creations--Cheesecake, Shrimp Bisque, Strawberry Tarts, Barbecued Spare Ribs, Tangy Pot Roast with Vegetables.

But cooking isn't all fun. It's also serious business. Once I realized I had total responsibility for the food my family ate, I knew I wanted to cook dishes that were good for them as well as good tasting.

For years, I was an advocate of low fat cooking. But recently I've changed my mind. It's been a long time since I've been able to lose any weight on a low fat diet. And even as I strictly controlled our fat intake, I watched my cholesterol and my blood pressure go up, along with my husband's cholesterol and triglycerides.

When my sister-in-law and a good friend began urging me to try lo-carb cooking, I resisted at first. Then I decided to give it a try.

With the approval of both our doctors, my husband and I have been restricting our carbohydrate intake for over a year now. We've both lost about 20 pounds and kept it off. What's more, his triglycerides went from 350 to 60--an astonishing improvement. My blood pressure is now back to normal. And we've also improved our HDL/LDL ratio significantly, although I know that part of the shift is due to our exercise schedule. (We both try to do 30 minutes of aerobics 4 or 5 days a week, and I also lift weights at the local athletic club twice a week.)

If you're reading this book, you've probably decided that lo-carb is the way for you to go. You may be interested in this eating plan because you want to lose weight. Or you may find it works for you over the long haul as a way to control both your weight and your cholesterol. One thing I love about this way of cooking is that if I do put on a pound or two, I can drop them almost instantly by cutting back on carbs.

There are many lo-carb diets, of course. Atkins, Protein Power, Sugar Busters, the Schwarzbein Principle. I've kept them all in mind when designing my recipes.

Critics have called a lo-carb diet boring. It certainly cuts out many familiar components of the American diet: pasta, rice, potatoes, bread, muffins, pastries. But that doesn't mean it's no fun.

You may have to look the other way when you see a banana muffin, but you sure can tuck into all the steak with bearnaise sauce, lobster, prime ribs, and beef stroganoff you want.

Frankly I don't think it takes a degree from the Culinary Institute of America to make lo-carb food that tastes good. How can you miss when your diet includes unlimited quantities of butter, bacon, cream, cheese, olive oil, steak, eggs, meat, fish and poultry?

The problem comes with variety. Even filet mignon will make your eyes glaze over if you have it every day. To keep a lo-carb eating plan interesting, you need lots of tasty appetizers, snacks, salads, vegetable dishes, main dishes and desserts.

That's where *Fabulous Lo-Carb Cuisine* comes in. I've been designing recipes for special diets for almost 20 years, and when I turned my thoughts to lo-carb cooking, I started coming up with a whole host of wonderful dishes: from Barbecued Spare Ribs and Middle Eastern Chicken to sinfully rich coffee Ice Cream and Mocha Pie. With this book, I haven't tried to create a compendium with tons of recipes-- some of which I'd inevitably liked better than others. Instead, I set my sights on producing a smaller book filled with great-tasting, easy to prepare dishes I can cook on a daily basis.

One of my approaches was to find ways to make the foods I like to eat. Take pizza, for example. You might think it's impossible to make a lo-carb pizza. But I've figured out a way to do it. Another of my recipe conversions is Kung Pao Chicken. Made the standard way, it's quite high in carbs. But I've been able to modify the traditional Szechuan recipe so it's perfect for our diet.

If I can't convert a dish, I think about some other way to achieve results I like. I probably won't be eating roast chicken with stuffing any time soon. But I can use the same flavor combination in a chicken salad or on chicken wings, for example.

I also love lasagna, and I've made one with thin sheets of phyllo dough instead of noodles. In addition, I've taken the time to develop sauces, dressings, and butters that will enhance other foods. Flavored butters are great on meat, fish, and vegetables. And my lo-carb versions of traditional favorites like cocktail sauce, and barbecue sauce are mainstays in my kitchen.

Desserts are important to staying on any eating plan. The good news is that there are many that are easy to make and so low in carbs that you can have them whenever you want.

Cheesecake is a natural, since you don't even have to vary the recipe much. Then there's my wonderful Fruit Pizza with a Marzipan Crust. And the ice cream I can whip up in half an hour is another standard around my house.

Incidentally, there are some lo-carb diets that forbid any use of white flour. Making a distinction between "good" carbs and "bad" carbs reminds me of the health food advocates in the 60's and 70's who bragged that they didn't use any sugar. Instead they sweetened their tea and baked goods with honey and concentrated apple juice--both excellent sources of sugar.

I put avoiding white flour in the same category. True, it's

got a lot of carbs. But if I need a tablespoon of flour to thicken my shrimp bisque, I use it. And if I can utilize a thin phyllo leaf to make a great main dish or a dessert, I'll use this, too.

You may already know that as far as lo-carb cooking is concerned, the sweetener problem has been solved by the Johnson and Johnson company, with Splenda. It's made from sugar--only with some changes in the molecular structure, which reduces the calorie and carbohydrate content to almost zero.

I've used Splenda in all of my desserts and many of my other dishes. Although it doesn't behave exactly like sugar in every recipe, it's close enough to make a great substitute in most cases.

ABOUT MY RECIPES

There are several important things I want to tell you about my recipes. I test them until I'm satisfied with the results and satisfied that someone else can easily follow my directions. So I usually start by developing a dish--then have one of my professional cooks test it in my home kitchen to make sure everything works the way it should. Along the way, I pass out samples to friends and family and get their opinion on the results.

Generally, I prefer to cook fresh ingredients. But if there's a convenience food that will simplify a dish--I use it. One of my most useful finds, for example, is flavored canned tomato sauce. Since it's already got the spices incorporated, you don't have to add a lot of seasonings.

Another real convenience is frozen pepper and onion stir fry--which saves the time of cutting the vegetables up. And instead of fooling with garlic cloves, I buy it already chopped.

For the most part, I've used ingredients that you can get at the grocery store. But you might have to visit a specialty shop for a few things like rice wine vinegar or hot oil, for my Kung Pao Chicken, for example. I also check the labels on products and use the ones with the lowest carb grams. If you get into the habit of reading labels, you'll find that some seemingly similar products are quite different in carb content, often due to the amount of added sugar.

When designing my recipes, I've kept in mind today's busy lifestyles. All of my dishes are easy to prepare, and I've tried to minimize the number of ingredients and also streamline directions.

NUTRITIONAL ANALYSIS
AND RECIPE YIELD

Recipe yield is an extremely important issue in a cookbook that makes nutritional claims. I've seen cookbooks that manipulate nutritional results by providing ridiculously small serving sizes.

I've tried to be realistic about servings, basing them on what my family and friends would actually eat at one sitting. If I think a pie really serves 8, for example, I'm not going to make it look as if it has fewer carbs by telling you it makes 12 tiny servings.

On the other hand, there are some dishes where the portions are larger than would traditionally be expected. In savory recipes, I might be using a pound of meat or more to serve 2 people. That's because a lo-carb dinner entree will probably be heavy on meat and light on vegetables. I'm not going to tell you a recipe with 4 pounds of meat serves 12. In a lo-carb diet it should only serve 7 or 8. *So, if you're assessing the carbs in my recipes and those in other books, please take the serving sizes into consideration*—so you won't be comparing apples with oranges, as they say.

With sauces, dressings, and butters, I give you the total amount (1 cup, for example) then suggest a serving size.

If there's a range of servings, say 4-6, the analysis will be based on the lower number--to give you as realistic a nutritional picture as possible.

All of my recipes have been nutritionally analyzed by a registered dietitian. Although I own the software to do this analysis myself and often do a quick check of a dish to see if I need to alter it for carb content, I know from past experience that working with a nutrition professional ensures accuracy.

Remember, when you check the nutritional content at the end of each recipe, that the effective amount of carbs in each dish is the amount of carbs minus the amount of fiber, since fiber is carbohydrate that is not absorbed by the body. For example, my Kung Pao Chicken has 10.6 grams of carbohydrate. But since it has 3.6 grams of dietary fiber, only 7 grams (i.e., 10.6 minus 3.6) are absorbed.

Another important point is that for herbs and spices, the USDA nutritional database almost exclusively lists nutritional values for ground herbs. In this cookbook, I have used many dried herb leaves such as thyme, basil, and tarragon. In recipes where these herb leaves are used, the nutritional analysis will be slightly higher in carbs than the actual dish. This is because ground herbs are more dense and thus have more carbs than a like quantity of herb leaves. For example, a teaspoon of ground basil has 0.9 grams of carbs. My guess is that a teaspoon of dried basil leaves has about half the carb grams. However, there is no way to know for sure, since they're not listed in small quantities on any database that I have discovered.

But the bottom line is, of course, taste. So dip into my book. I think I've come up with over 100 choice recipes--dishes that enhance the eating pleasure of my family and friends. Frozen Strawberry Pie, Southwestern Quiche, Cream of Tomato Soup, Portobello Slices, Parsley-Lemon Butter, Almond Chicken Salad, Pizza. Foods you'll love to eat, and foods that make it easy to stay on a lo-carb diet.

CHAPTER 1
Brilliant Beginnings

There's nothing I like better than fixing food for a party, which means that over the years I've made a specialty of creating appetizers and hors d'oeuvres like Hot Artichoke and Spinach Dip, Spanakopita Bake, and Spicy Cocktail Hotdogs that friends and family can enjoy in bite-sized portions.

Of course, there's good news and bad news about lo-carb appetizers. You can use all the "fattening" ingredients that you felt guilty about eating before. But you can't serve them on bread or crackers. In place of high-carb accompaniments, I've used vegetables such as celery and pepper sticks and Belgian endive. Another approach is to simply transfer some Chopped Liver, Blue Cheese Ball, or Chili Con Queso to a plate and eat it with a fork.

One fun section of this chapter features several recipes for Chicken Wings–which make excellent party food. The method I've developed for cooking them is so easy that when I'm in the mood for wings, I often serve them as a main course for dinner.

In addition, since I love soups, I've also included several here, such as Cream of Tomato Soup and Shrimp Bisque, that are quite low in carbs.

You'll also find a pizza and a quesadilla–both made with La Tortilla lo-carb tortillas. (See Page 136 for buying information.)

Shrimp Bisque

There are so many "fancy" dishes that you've probably had in restaurants but never thought of making at home. Here's a wonderful example: Shrimp Bisque that goes from stove to table in minutes. For a pretty presentation, reserve 1 shrimp per serving. Float the shrimp in the center of the soup bowl, surrounded by a light sprinkling of chopped parsley.

Makes 2 or 3 servings

2 Tbsp butter
1 Tbsp white flour
1 cup heavy cream
1 cup chicken broth
Dash garlic powder
Dash white pepper
2 cups chopped cooked shrimp.
2 or 3 shrimp and chopped fresh parsley for garnish
        (optional)

1. In a heavy, medium saucepan, melt the butter over medium heat. Stir in the flour until well blended. Gradually pour in the cream, stirring until the mixture thickens. Slowly add the chicken broth, continuing to stir.
2. Stir in the garlic powder and pepper. Stir in the shrimp. Raise heat, stirring, so that soup becomes hot. Reduce heat to medium low, and heat 2 or 3 minutes to allow flavors to blend. Garnish each serving with a whole shrimp and/or chopped parsley, if desired.

Carbs: 7 g   Protein: 39.6 g   Calories: 715.9   Fiber: 0.1 g

Cream of Tomato Soup

If you're craving tomato soup, this version won't spoil your carb count for the day.

Makes 2 servings

1/4 cup plus 1 Tbsp tomato sauce
1/2 cup chicken broth
1/4 cup heavy cream
1/4 cup half and half

1. In a small saucepan, combine tomato sauce, broth, cream, and half and half. Stir to mix well. Warm over medium to medium-low heat. Do not boil. Serve in cups.

Carbs: 5.1 g   Protein: 2.5 g   Calories: 160.8   Fiber: 0.5 g

Cream of Tomato-Chili Soup

For an easy variation, make Cream of Tomato Soup; then stir in 2 or 3 tablespoons of mild chopped canned green chilis with the other ingredients.

Carbs: 5.6 g   Protein: 2.5 g   Calories: 163.3   Fiber: 1 g

Cauliflower Cheese Soup

I love the marriage of cauliflower and cheese in this easy but opulent soup.

Makes 2 to 3 servings

1 cup chicken broth
1 1/2 cups diced cauliflower florets.
Dash garlic powder
Dash white pepper
2 Tbsp butter
1 Tbsp white flour
3/4 cup heavy cream
3 Tbsp grated Parmesan cheese

1. In a small saucepan, combine broth, cauliflower, garlic powder, and pepper. Bring to a boil. Cover, reduce heat, and simmer 4 or 5 minutes until cauliflower is tender.
2. Meanwhile, in heavy, medium saucepan over medium heat, melt the butter. Stir in the flour until well blended. Gradually pour in the cream, stirring until the mixture thickens, about 2 minutes. Slowly add the cooked cauliflower mixture, continuing to stir.
3. Reduce heat to low and stir in the cheese.

Carbs: 10.2 g   Protein: 8 g   Calories: 497.7   Fiber: 2 g

New England Clam Chowder

Here's rich and creamy clam chowder. By the way, while I usually use dried thyme leaves in recipes, this one calls for ground thyme because without thickener, thyme leaves tend to float to the top of the soup.

Makes 3 or 4 servings

1/2 cup chopped onion
3 bacon strips, cut into 3/4-in pieces
2 Tbsp butter
2 6 1/2-oz cans minced clams, including juice
Water
1 cup diced cauliflower florets
1/8 tsp ground thyme
Dash white pepper
1 cup heavy cream
Salt to taste (optional)
2 Tbsp chopped fresh parsley leaves for garnish

1. In a large heavy saucepan over medium heat, cook onion and bacon in butter, stirring frequently, until onion is tender and bacon is crisp, about 11 or 12 minutes. If bacon sticks to bottom of pot, reduce heat.
2. Meanwhile, drain clams and reserve liquid in a 2-cup measure. Add enough water to clam liquid to make 1 1/4 cups.
3. Drain off and discard fat. Add liquid to pot, scraping up any brown bits from pot bottom. Add clams, cauliflower, thyme and white pepper. Stir to mix. Bring to a boil, reduce heat, cover and simmer until cauliflower is tender and flavors are blended, about 8 minutes.
4. Stir in cream. Heat, but do not boil. Add salt if desired. Garnish with parsley.

Carbs: 6.6 g   Protein: 5.2 g   Calories: 403.8   Fiber: 1.4 g

Hot Artichoke and Spinach Dip

There are many classic hot dips and spreads that you may have enjoyed at a restaurant and wondered if you could duplicate them at home. Here's a great example. The combination of flavors and textures always makes this appetizer a hit at parties. Keep it warm on a hot tray, or simply return it to the microwave for a minute or 2 when the spread begins to cool down.

Makes 36 servings, 2 tsp each

6 or 7 artichoke heart quarters
2/3 cup commercial sour cream
1/3 cup grated Parmesan cheese
1 3-oz package cream cheese, at room temperature
2 tsp instant minced onions
1/2 tsp chopped garlic
3 or 4 drops hot pepper sauce
1/4 tsp salt
1/4 cup thawed and drained cut leaf frozen spinach

1. Remove and discard any tough outer leaves from the artichoke hearts. Coarsely chop hearts. Set aside.
2. In a medium bowl, combine sour cream, Parmesan cheese, cream cheese, onion, garlic, hot pepper sauce, and salt. Stir with a fork until well blended. Stir in artichoke hearts and spinach. Transfer to a small glass or ceramic microwave-safe, casserole or bowl. Cover with casserole lid or wax paper, and microwave on high power for 3 or 4 minutes, or until heated through. Serve hot with celery sticks, red and green pepper sticks or Belgian endive leaves. Leftover dip will keep in the refrigerator for 2 or 3 days.

Carbs: 0.6 g   Protein: 0.8 g   Calories: 21.4   Fiber: 0 g

Chili Con Queso Dip

Mexican food has always been one of our favorites. While many of the ingredients don't work well on a lo-carb eating plan, it is possible to come up with some satisfying flavor combinations. In fact, here's one of my favorite crowd-pleasers, updated for lo-carb cooking. Serve on small plates, or use celery and other cut vegetables to dip up portions of the meat and cheese mixture.

Makes 120 servings, 2 tsp each

1 lb lean ground beef
1 medium onion, chopped
1 tsp chopped garlic
1 16-oz jar mild salsa
2 tsp Splenda
1 tsp chili powder
1 tsp ground cumin
1/2 tsp salt, or to taste
1 8-oz package grated sharp Cheddar cheese

1. In a small Dutch oven or large pot, combine the ground beef, onion, and garlic. Cook over medium heat until the beef is browned, 5 or 6 minutes.
2. Add the salsa, Splenda, chili powder, cumin, and salt. Stir to mix well. Bring to a boil, reduce heat, cover and simmer 15 minutes, stirring frequently, to allow the flavors to blend. Remove from heat. Stir in cheese until melted.
3. Serve warm in a chafing dish or on a hot plate. Leftovers keep 3 or 4 days in the refrigerator covered. Reheat in the microwave.

Carbs: 0.5 g   Protein: 1.3 g   Calories: 17.2   Fiber: 0.1 g

Spanakopita Bake

Because it's so thin, frozen phyllo dough is very low in carbs and works well for creating a variety of pastries. Here I've used it in a Greek-style spinach and cheese bake. Allow 5 hours to thaw frozen phyllo at room temperature. If you forget to thaw the dough, you can do it in the microwave. However, sheets of microwave-thawed dough may stick together in some places, making them harder to work with. Use a pastry brush to spread the butter on the phyllo sheets.

Makes 54 servings

2 Tbsp olive oil
1 cup chopped onion
1 1-lb bag cut leaf frozen spinach
2 1/2 tsp dried dill weed
1/4 tsp salt, or to taste
1/4 tsp black pepper
12 oz crumbled feta cheese
1 32-oz carton ricotta cheese
2 large eggs, slightly beaten
3 large phyllo sheets, thawed
1/3 cup melted butter

1. Preheat the oven to 375 degrees.
2. In a large skillet over medium heat, combine the oil and onion. Cook the onion, stirring frequently, until it is soft but not browned. Stir in the spinach. Cover and cook gently for 4 or 5 minutes, stirring occasionally, and breaking up any large lumps of spinach if necessary
3. Remove the skillet from the burner. Stir in the dill, salt, pepper, and cheeses. Stir in the eggs. Spread melted butter in the bottom of an 8 1/2- by 11-inch baking pan.
4. Unwrap the phyllo onto wax paper. Cover with additional wax paper and a barely damp tea towel. Working quickly, cut 3 large sheets in half at the folded edge. Lay one of

these half phyllo sheets in the bottom of the pan. Spread with melted butter. Add 2 more half sheets, spreading each with butter. Cover with the filling, spreading the mixture evenly with the back of a large spoon or spatula. Top with 3 half phyllo sheets, brushing each layer with the melted butter.

5. Bake for about 35 to 37 minutes or until the filling is cooked through and the top layer of phyllo begins to brown. Serve at once, or cover and refrigerate up to 24 hours before serving. Warm in a 350-degree oven for about 20 minutes. Cut into 54 squares to serve. Leftovers will keep in the refrigerator 2 or 3 days and can be reheated in the microwave.

Carbs: 2.1 g   Protein: 3.4 g   Calories: 70.3   Fiber: 0.3 g

Spicy Cocktail Hotdogs

Use toothpicks to spear these yummy little bites. If you like, you can broil the hotdogs before cutting them into serving pieces, but cutting them first gives the ends a plump, inviting look.

Makes 30 servings

1 Tbsp Dijon-style mustard
1 Tbsp light soy sauce
1 Tbsp plus 1 tsp Splenda
1 tsp cider vinegar
1 pkg kosher hotdogs, cut into bite-sized pieces

1. In a small bowl, stir together mustard, soy sauce, Splenda, and vinegar.
2. Lay hotdogs on a baking sheet covered with aluminum foil. Spread half of sauce over top. Broil 4 inches from heat 2 or 3 minutes, until hotdogs begin to brown and puff up. Turn hotdogs and spread with remaining sauce. Broil an additional 2 or 3 minutes. Serve warm

Carbs: 0.4 g   Protein: 1.9 g   Calories: 35.9   Fiber: 0 g

Teriyaki Wings

Chicken wings make delightful party food. Here teriyaki sauce gives them an irresistible flavor.

Makes about 24 servings

1/4 cup light soy sauce
2 Tbsp peanut oil
2 Tbsp Chinese cooking wine or dry sherry
1 tsp Splenda
3/4 tsp ground ginger
1 tsp chopped garlic
2 1/4 lb chicken wings

1. In a large bowl or ceramic casserole, mix together soy sauce, oil, wine, Splenda, ginger, and garlic. Reserve.
2. With a sharp knife, cut wing tips from wings and discard. Disjoint wings and place them in bowl with reserved marinade. Stir to coat. Cover and refrigerate 2 or 3 hours or up to 12 hours, stirring occasionally.
3. Transfer wings and marinade to a 9 1/2- by 13-inch baking pan. Broil about 4 inches from heat, turning wings and basting occasionally with sauce for 17 to 20 minutes until wings are cooked through and begin to brown. Serve warm. Wings can be cooked ahead and reheated in the broiler or microwave.

Carbs: 0.3 g   Protein: 4.6 g   Calories: 59.4   Fiber: 0 g

Buffalo Wings

One of my all-time favorite appetizers, these wings are so easy to make that I often serve them for dinner with a salad. Each brand of hot sauce has its own distinctive flavor. You may want to experiment with various products to find out which you like best.

Makes 30 servings

3 1/2 lb chicken wings
1/4 cup butter, melted
1/2 cup hot pepper sauce such as Tabasco
1/2 Tbsp white vinegar.

1. Preheat broiler. Cut wing tips from wings and discard. Cut wings apart at joint, and place them in a 9 1/2- by 13-inch baking pan.
2. In a small bowl, Mix together butter, hot sauce, and vinegar. Pour over wings, and stir to coat.
3. Broil about 4 inches from heat, turning wings and basting 3 or 4 times with sauce, for 20 to 25 minutes until wings are cooked through and begin to crisp and brown. Serve warm with blue cheese dressing and celery sticks. Wings can be cooked ahead and reheated in the broiler or microwave.

Carbs: 0.1 g   Protein: 5.5 g   Calories: 72.4   Fiber: 0 g

Spicy "Honey" Mustard Wings

The combination of flavors in this tangy and delicious sauce makes these wings taste like they're made with honey as well as mustard.

Makes 30 servings

1/2 cup prepared (yellow) mustard
1/4 cup cider vinegar
1/4 cup tomato sauce
1/4 cup Splenda
1/2 Tbsp Worcestershire sauce
1/2 Tbsp soy sauce
1 tsp hot pepper sauce
3 1/2 lb chicken wings

1. In a large bowl or ceramic casserole, mix together mustard, vinegar, tomato sauce, Splenda, Worcestershire sauce, soy sauce, and hot pepper sauce. Reserve.
2. With a sharp knife, cut wing tips from wings and discard. Disjoint wings and place them in bowl with marinade. Stir to coat. Cover and refrigerate 2 or 3 hours or up to 12 hours, stirring occasionally.
3. Transfer wings and marinade to a 9 1/2- by 13-inch baking pan. Broil about 4 inches from heat, turning wings and basting occasionally with sauce, for 20 to 25 minutes until wings are cooked through and begin to brown. Serve warm. Wings can be cooked ahead and reheated in the broiler or microwave.

Carbs: 0.6 g   Protein: 5.5 g   Calories: 64   Fiber: 0.1 g

Wings with Poultry Seasoning

Simple but delicious.

Makes about 24 servings

1/4 cup cider vinegar
3 Tbsp olive oil
1 tsp chopped garlic
1 tsp poultry seasoning
1/4 tsp salt
1/8 tsp black pepper
2 1/4 lb chicken wings

1. In a large bowl or ceramic casserole, mix together vinegar, oil, garlic, poultry seasoning, salt, and pepper. Reserve.
2. With a sharp knife, cut wing tips from wings and discard. Disjoint wings and place them in bowl with reserved marinade. Stir to coat. Cover and refrigerate 2 or 3 hours or up to 12 hours, stirring occasionally.
3. Transfer wings and marinade to a 9 1/2- by 13-inch baking pan. Broil about 4 inches from heat, turning wings and basting occasionally with sauce, for 17 to 20 minutes until wings are cooked through and begin to brown. Serve warm. Wings can be cooked ahead and reheated in the broiler or microwave.

Carbs: 0.2 g   Protein: 4.3 g   Calories: 62.2   Fiber: 0 g

Mini Crab Cakes

Without breading, crab cakes must be small in order to hold together. Although I've made these spicy little cakes in appetizer portions, you can also make them the centerpiece of a meal. Serve with the Cocktail Sauce on Page 64 or the Louie Dressing on Page 60.

Makes 4 servings

1 egg, lightly beaten
1 Tbsp mayonnaise
1 Tbsp heavy cream
1 1/4 tsp Old Bay seasoning, or to taste
8 oz back fin or lump crab meat
3 Tbsp butter

1. In a medium bowl, mix together egg, mayonnaise, cream, and Old Bay seasoning. With fingers or a fork, work in crab meat just until blended.
2. Shape into 8 small cakes. Melt butter over medium heat in a large non-stick skillet. Add crab cakes to pan, and saute, turning once with 1 or 2 plastic spatulas, until golden and crisp on the outside. Transfer to a serving plate.

Carbs: 0.3 g   Protein: 12.7 g   Calories: 192.1   Fiber: 0 g

Crab Dunk

Rich and tangy. This one's a slam dunk.

Makes 1 1/2 cups (36 2-tsp servings)

1/2 cup whipped cream cheese
1/2 cup mayonnaise
2 Tbsp lemon juice
1 tsp Worcestershire sauce
1 tsp chopped garlic
1/2 tsp dry mustard
1/2 tsp celery salt
3 to 4 drops hot pepper sauce
8 oz back fin or lump crab meat
1/4 cup chopped chives or minced green onion tops

1. In a small, microwave-safe casserole, combine cream cheese and mayonnaise. Whisk until smooth. Whisk in lemon juice, Worcestershire sauce, garlic, mustard, celery salt, and hot pepper sauce, and stir with a fork until well combined. Stir in crab meat and chives.
2. Serve with celery sticks, broccoli, cauliflower, or slices of red and green pepper. Dip will keep in the refrigerator for 1 or 2 days.

Carbs: 0.2 g   Protein: 1.3 g   Calories: 40.4   Fiber: 0 g

Quesadilla

La Tortilla makes whole wheat tortillas that are very low in carbs. I've used one in this recipe to make a quesadilla which I eat for a snack or for breakfast. Buying information is on Page 136.

Makes 1 serving

1 La Tortilla tortilla
1/3 cup shredded Cheddar or jack cheese
1 Tbsp mild or medium salsa

1. Lay tortilla on a medium microwave-safe plate. Sprinkle evenly with cheese. Microwave on full power 35 to 40 seconds, just until cheese is melted.
2. Spread salsa over cheese on half of the tortilla. Fold in half and eat.

Carbs: 13.3 g   Protein: 14.6 g   Calories: 215.5   Fiber: 9.2 g

White Pizza

If you like white pizza (with no tomato sauce), here's a super-quick version. It's made on a La Tortilla tortilla. By the way, I've cheated and included an orange cheese with the white ones, so you could buy them all already grated or shredded. For tortilla buying information see Page 136.

Makes 1 serving

1 La Tortilla tortilla.
Generous 1/8 tsp Italian seasoning
Dash garlic powder
3 Tbsp shredded mozzarella cheese
3 Tbsp shredded Cheddar cheese
1/2 Tbsp grated Parmesan cheese
2 tsp finely chopped red onion

1. Preheat broiler. Lay the tortilla on a small baking sheet or piece of aluminum foil. Sprinkle the Italian seasoning and garlic powder over the tortilla.
2. Sprinkle on the cheese. Sprinkle with the onion.
3. Broil about 4 inches from heat until the cheese has melted and the edges of the tortilla begin to crisp, about 2 to 2 1/2 minutes.

Carbs: 15.3 g   Protein: 32.2 g   Calories: 391.5   Fiber: 9.1 g

Artichoke and Shrimp Dip

A winning combination—artichokes and shrimp.

Makes 42 servings, 2 tsp each

6 or 7 canned artichoke heart quarters
1/3 lb cooked and ready to eat medium shrimp (about 1 1/4
    cups)
1 3-oz pkg cream cheese, softened
1/3 cup mayonnaise
1 tsp instant minced onions
1/2 tsp chopped garlic
1/2 tsp dried thyme leaves
1/2 tsp dried basil leaves
1/2 tsp lemon juice
1/8 tsp salt, or to taste
1/8 tsp white pepper

1. Remove and discard the coarse outer leaves from the
   artichoke hearts. In a food processor bowl, combine the
   shrimp and artichoke hearts. Process with on and off
   bursts just until coarsely chopped. Set aside.
2. In a small bowl, with a fork, mash and stir together the
   cream cheese and mayonnaise until well combined.
3. Stir in the onion, garlic, thyme, basil, lemon juice, salt, and
   pepper; mix well. Stir in the artichokes and shrimp.

4. Cover and refrigerate at least 1/2 hours and up to 12 hours to allow flavors to blend. Serve with celery sticks, Belgian endive leaves, red and green pepper sticks. Leftover dip can be refrigerated 1 or 2 days if very fresh shrimp have been used.

Carbs: 0.4 g   Protein: 1 g   Calories: 25   Fiber: 0 g

Chopped Liver

Rich and robust, chopped liver is definitely on the lo-carb menu.

Makes 8 servings, 1/4 cup each

1 lb chicken livers, rinsed
3 large eggs, rinsed
1/4 cup mayonnaise
2 tsp instant minced onions
1/4 tsp salt, or to taste
Dash black pepper

1. In a medium saucepan, combine liver and eggs. Cover with cool water. Over high heat, bring to a boil. Cover, reduce heat, and boil 20 minutes, or until liver is cooked through.
2. Transfer liver and eggs to a colander, and cool slightly under running water. Drain well.
3. Peel eggs and cut into large pieces. Combine eggs and liver in a food processor bowl. Process with on and off bursts just until liver and eggs are coarsely chopped. Do not over-process. Transfer to a medium bowl. Stir in mayonnaise, onion, salt, and pepper. Stir to mix well. Cover and refrigerate 30 minutes and up to several hours until flavors are blended.
4. Serve on a plate or with celery sticks and Belgian endive leaves. Chopped liver will keep in the refrigerator 2 or 3 days.

Carbs: 0.9 g   Protein: 11 g   Calories: 135   Fiber: 0 g

Salmon Spread

Always a big hit at parties.

Makes 2 1/8 cups

1 14 1/2-oz can red salmon, drained
1/4 cup mayonnaise
1 3-oz package cream cheese cut into 3 or 4 pieces
1 Tbsp lemon juice
1 tsp instant minced onion
3/4 tsp dried dill weed
1 tsp prepared white horseradish
1/4 tsp salt, or to taste
3 or 4 drops hot pepper sauce
1/2 cup finely chopped pecans, divided
2 Tbsp finely chopped fresh parsley leaves

1. Remove skin and bones from salmon and discard. Break salmon into small pieces. Set aside in a medium bowl.
2. In a food processor bowl, combine the salmon, mayonnaise, cream cheese, lemon juice, onion, dill, horseradish, salt, and hot pepper sauce. Process until almost completely smooth. Stir in about half the pecans.
3. Turn out mixture onto a piece of plastic wrap. Using plastic wrap to keep spread from sticking to fingers, mold into a rounded shape, and set on a small serving plate. Remove plastic wrap. Coat surface of spread with parsley and remaining nuts.
4. Chill 2 or 3 hours before serving. Serve with celery sticks, Belgian endive, and red and green pepper sticks.

Carbs: 0.3 g   Protein: 3 g   Calories: 42   Fiber: 0.1 g

Favorite Deviled Eggs

I used to feel guilty about eating deviled eggs, but not on this diet! This recipe does have some zip. If you like your deviled eggs more bland, reduce the relish and mustard slightly.

Makes 6 servings

6 large eggs, hard boiled
1/4 cup mayonnaise
2 tsp dill relish
1/2 tsp Splenda
1/2 tsp Dijon-style mustard
Sliced green pimiento olives or paprika for garnish (optional)

1. Peel eggs and carefully cut in half.
2. Remove yolks and transfer to a medium bowl. Set egg white halves on a large plate. Mash yolks with fork tines. Stir in mayonnaise, relish, Splenda, and mustard. Return yolk mixture to egg white halves, dividing evenly. If desired, garnish with a slice of pimiento olive or paprika. Serve at once, or cover and refrigerate. Deviled eggs will keep in the refrigerator for 2 or 3 days.

Carbs: 0.8 g   Protein: 6.3 g   Calories: 142   Fiber: 0 g

Cheddar Cheese and Olive Spread

Using whipped cream cheese lowers the amount of carbs in this festive and flavorful cheese spread.

Makes 2 cups (48 2-tsp servings)

1 8-oz tub whipped cream cheese
2 cups shredded Cheddar cheese
1/4 tsp Worcestershire sauce
3 or 4 drops hot pepper sauce
1/4 cup chopped green pimiento olives
1 tsp instant minced onions

1. In a food processor bowl, combine cream cheese, Cheddar, Worcestershire sauce, and hot pepper sauce. Process until well combined, stopping and scraping down the sides of the bowl as necessary. Remove to a medium bowl. Stir in the olives and minced onion. Transfer to a crock or small bowl. Cover with plastic wrap, and refrigerate 1 or 2 hours until flavors are well blended. Serve with celery sticks and red and green pepper sticks. Spread will keep in the refrigerator for up to 10 days.

Carbs: 0.3 g   Protein: 1.5 g   Calories: 36.8   Fiber: 0 g

Blue Cheese Ball

Always a hit, this cheese ball has a mild blue cheese flavor and the crunch of pecans and celery.

Makes 36 servings, 2 tsp each

1 8-oz tub whipped cream cheese
1/3 cup crumbled blue cheese
1 medium stalk celery, finely diced
1/2 cup finely chopped pecans, divided
1 tsp instant minced onions
Dash garlic powder
1/8 tsp salt

1. In a medium bowl, combine the cheeses, celery, half the pecans, onion, garlic powder, and salt. Stir with a fork to mix well. With fingers, mold into a ball. Coat the ball with the remaining pecans. Cover with plastic wrap, and refrigerate 1 or 2 hours. Cheese ball will keep in the refrigerator for up to a week. Serve with celery sticks and red and green pepper sticks or Belgian endive.

Carbs: 0.5 g   Protein: 0.8 g   Calories: 37   Fiber: 0.2 g

Peanut Butter and "Marmalade" Spread

If peanut butter and jelly is comfort food for you, here's a reasonable substitute that I concocted one afternoon when I'd come home from the dentist and the Novocaine hadn't worn off. I wanted something good to eat that I didn't have to chew, so I made this spread. I ate it with a spoon, but you could put it on a celery stick.

Makes 2 servings

2 Tbsp old-fashioned peanut butter
1 Tbsp Splenda
Scant 1/4 tsp orange extract

1. Stir together all ingredients.

Carbs: 3.9 g   Protein: 4 g   Calories: 89.2   Fiber: 1.3 g

CHAPTER 2
Gourmet Greens

Salads and vegetables are a natural part of a lo-carb eating plan, if you pick the right ones. All the green, leafy salad ingredients are excellent choices. Other good selections include broccoli, cauliflower, green beans, celery, peppers, radishes, olives, mushrooms, cabbage, and zucchini. Happily, many of these are the vegetables richest in vitamins and minerals.

In this chapter I've provided a selection of tempting salads and vegetable dishes. Some, such as my Mexican Salad; Steak Salad; Broccoli, Ham, and Cheese Salad; Bacon and Tuna Salad; Chicken Salad with Almonds; and Cauliflower and Cheese, are actually hearty enough to be main dishes. Others, like Roasted Asparagus, Marinated Vegetables, Brazilian Green Beans, and Portobello Slices are designed to round out a meal.

Many of these dishes are perfect for a buffet table along with the main dishes you'll find in a later chapter.

By the way, when I want to duplicate the convenience of a sandwich, I'll put one of my chunky salads—like Broccoli-Ham Salad or Chicken-Broccoli-Almond Salad— into half a green pepper.

Mexican Salad

Taco salad—without the tacos.

Makes 3 or 4 servings

3/4 pound lean ground beef
1 tsp chopped garlic
1/3 cup mild salsa
1 tsp chili powder
1/4 tsp salt, or to taste
3 Tbsp mild salsa
3 Tbsp olive oil
1 Tbsp cider vinegar
2 tsp Splenda
7 cups mixed salad greens
1 1/2 cups grated sharp Cheddar cheese
1/4 cup diced tomato
1/4 cup diced sweet red pepper

1. In a large saucepan, combine the ground beef and garlic. Cook over medium heat until the beef is browned, 5 or 6 minutes.
2. Add the 1/3 cup salsa, chili powder, and salt, and mix well. Reduce heat, cover, and cook 8 to 10 minutes, stirring frequently. Remove from heat.
3. Meanwhile, in a large bowl, combine the 3 tablespoons salsa, oil, vinegar, and Splenda. Stir to mix well. Add the salad greens, and toss to coat. Add the cheese, tomato, and pepper. Toss to coat. Add the meat, and toss to combine. Serve immediately.

Carbs: 8.5 g   Protein: 36.5 g   Calories: 605.2   Fiber: 3.2 g

Steak Salad, Greek-Style

Greek salad with steak—a wonderful combination. I cook the steak on my George Foreman grill while I'm preparing the rest of the ingredients.

Makes 3 or 4 servings

1 lb sirloin steak
Salt and pepper to taste
1/4 cup olive oil
1 Tbsp red wine vinegar
1/2 tsp dried thyme leaves
1/2 tsp dried basil leaves
1/4 cup crumbled feta cheese
6 cups mixed salad greens
1/2 to 3/4 cup oil-cured Greek olives, preferably seedless
1/4 cup chopped red onion
1/2 cup diced tomato

1. Sprinkle steak with salt and pepper. Broil or grill according to desired degree of doneness.
2. Meanwhile, In a large bowl, combine oil, vinegar, thyme, and basil. Stir to mix well. Stir in cheese. Add greens, olives, onion, and tomato. Toss to coat with dressing.
3. Cool steak slightly. Cut on the diagonal into strips. Toss with salad. Arrange salad on a large serving platter. Serve immediately.

Carbs: 7.8 g   Protein: 30.6 g   Calories: 419.6   Fiber: 3.3 g

Bacon, Lettuce, and Tomato Salad

If you yearn for a bacon, lettuce, and tomato sandwich, here's a salad that duplicates the taste combination. Incidentally, for an even quicker version of this dish, you can use a bag of already cut up lettuce.

Makes 2 servings

4 or 5 strips lean bacon
1/4 cup olive oil
1 Tbsp cider vinegar
3 Tbsp chopped red onion
4 cups torn romaine or iceberg lettuce leaves
1/2 cup diced tomato

1. In a large skillet, fry bacon over medium heat until crisp. With a slotted spoon, remove bacon from pan. When cool enough to handle, crumble and reserve.
2. In a large bowl combine the oil, vinegar, and onion. Stir to mix well. Stir in lettuce, reserved bacon, onion, and tomato. Serve. Salad will keep in the refrigerator for 1 or 2 days.

Carbs: 7 g   Protein: 6.3 g   Calories: 346.9   Fiber: 2.8 g

Broccoli, Ham, and Cheese Salad

You'll love the tangy flavor and interesting combination of ingredients in this salad.

Makes 4-5 servings

1/2 cup mayonnaise
2 Tbsp cider vinegar
1 1/2 Tbsp Splenda
3 cups small broccoli florets
3/4 lb cooked ham, diced
1 cup shredded Cheddar cheese
3 Tbsp chopped red onion

1. Place the mayonnaise in a large bowl; whisk in the vinegar and Splenda until well combined.
2. Add the broccoli, ham, cheese, and onion, and toss with the dressing. Serve at once, or refrigerate several hours before serving. Stir before serving. Salad will keep in the refrigerator 2 or 3 days.

Carbs: 5.5 g   Protein: 30.4 g   Calories: 471.9 Fiber: 2.1 g

Tuna-Bacon Salad

If you're looking for new flavor combinations, try this tuna-bacon salad. Fresh chives are a nice addition to the salad. If they're not available, substitute thinly sliced green onion tops. To speed preparation, use already prepared salad greens.

Makes 2 servings

4 or 5 strips lean bacon
1/4 cup olive oil
1 Tbsp cider vinegar
5 cups torn romaine or iceberg lettuce leaves
1 6 1/2-oz can water-packed tuna, drained and flaked
2 Tbsp chopped chives or thinly sliced green onion tops
1/2 cup diced tomato

1. In a large skillet, fry bacon over medium heat until bacon is crisp. With a slotted spoon, remove bacon from pan. When cool enough to handle, crumble and reserve.
2. Meanwhile, in a large bowl, combine the oil and vinegar. Stir to mix well. Stir in lettuce, reserved bacon, tuna, chives, and tomato. Serve. Salad will keep in the refrigerator 1 or 2 days.

Carbs: 6.5 g   Protein: 30.2 g   Calories: 453.4   Fiber: 3.1 g

Chicken-Broccoli-Almond Salad

I love the taste of poultry seasoning, which is usually used to flavor stuffing. Since bread cubes don't fit well into a lo-carb diet, I use the seasoning in this easy chicken salad. To speed the preparation, I buy already-roasted chicken. By the way, sauteing the almonds gives them a wonderful flavor and crisp texture.

Makes 4 servings

3/4 cup slivered almonds
1 Tbsp butter
3/4 cup mayonnaise
1 tsp poultry seasoning
1/8 tsp salt, or to taste
3 1/2 cups cooked chicken, cut into bite-sized pieces
3 cups small broccoli florets
3 Tbsp chopped red onion

1. In a large non-stick skillet over medium heat, saute almonds in butter, stirring constantly with a wooden spoon, until they turn golden brown, about 6 minutes. Reserve on a paper-towel-covered plate.
2. In a large bowl, whisk together the mayonnaise, poultry seasoning, and salt. Stir in chicken, broccoli, almonds, and onion.
3. Cover and refrigerate several hours or overnight. Salad will keep in the refrigerator 2 or 3 days.

Carbs: 7.9 g   Protein: 43.9 g   Calories: 681.9   Fiber: 4.1 g

Cauliflower Salad

Here's the perfect substitute for pasta or potato salad. If you like, you can parboil the cauliflower before adding it to the salad.

Makes 7 to 8 servings

3/4 cup mayonnaise
1 Tbsp Dijon-style mustard
2 Tbsp cider vinegar
1 Tbsp Splenda
1/4 tsp celery salt
7 or 8 cups small cauliflower florets
1/4 cup chopped red onion
1 red bell pepper, diced
1/4 cup chopped parsley leaves

1. In a large bowl, whisk together the mayonnaise, mustard, vinegar, Splenda, and celery salt.
2. Stir in the cauliflower, onion, pepper, and parsley. Serve at once, or refrigerate up to 24 hours before serving. Leftover salad will keep 2 or 3 days in the refrigerator.

Carbs: 7.2 g   Protein: 2.3 g   Calories: 206.4   Fiber: 2.9 g

Broccoli-Cauliflower-Pecan Salad

I first had a salad similar to this one in a little restaurant on the upper East side of Manhattan. I loved the marriage of nuts, broccoli, and cauliflower so much that I decided to duplicate the combination. If you like, you can omit the cauliflower and make the salad with 6 cups of broccoli.

Makes 6 servings

1/3 cup mayonnaise
1/3 cup commercial sour cream
1 tsp dried dill leaves
1/2 tsp celery salt
Dash white pepper
3 cups small broccoli florets and peeled stem pieces
3 cups small cauliflower florets
1 cup pecan halves
2 Tbsp chopped chives or green onion tops

1. In a medium bowl, whisk together mayonnaise, sour cream, dill, celery salt, and pepper.
2. Stir in broccoli, cauliflower, pecans, and chives. Serve at once, or cover and refrigerate up to 24 hours before serving. Salad will keep for 2 or 3 days in the refrigerator.

Carbs: 8.1 g   Protein: 4.7 g   Calories: 263.5   Fiber: 4.6 g

Cole Slaw

There are so many variations on the cole slaw theme. Here's a good one with a mayonnaise dressing. For an attractive presentation, combine red and green cabbage in the slaw.

Makes 7 or 8 servings

1 cup mayonnaise
2 Tbsp cider vinegar
1 1/2 Tbsp Splenda
1/2 tsp celery seed
10 cups chopped cabbage (preferably 2 cups red, 8 cups
      green)
1/4 cup red onion or chopped chives
1/2 cup sweet red pepper

1. In a large bowl, whisk together mayonnaise, vinegar, Splenda, and celery seed. Add the cabbage, onion, and pepper. Stir to mix well. Serve immediately or cover and refrigerate up to 24 hours before serving. Cole slaw will keep in the refrigerator 3 or 4 days.

Carbs: 6.9 g   Protein: 1.6 g   Calories: 259.6 Fiber: 2.5 g

Marinated Vegetables

The beauty of this marinated salad is that you can use primarily low-carb vegetables—with a sprinkling of higher-carb ones for added flavor. I make the salad with my Herb Dressing, Page 58. If you like, you can use a commercial Italian dressing, although you will be adding some carbs to the recipe. Also, you can parboil the cauliflower before adding it to the salad, if desired.

Makes 5 servings

1 cup coarsely chopped canned artichoke hearts, tough outer
   leaves removed
2 cups chopped cauliflower florets
3/4 cup oil-cured black olives
1/2 sweet red pepper, seeded and diced
1/4 cup sliced green onion tops
1/3 cup Herb Dressing (Page 58)

1. In a medium bowl, combine the artichoke hearts,
   cauliflower, olives, pepper, and onion.
2. Pour the dressing over the vegetables, and gently stir to mix
   well. Cover and refrigerate several hours or overnight
   before serving, stirring occasionally. Leftover salad will
   keep in the refrigerator 2 or 3 days.

Carbs: 8.1 g   Protein: 2.7 g   Calories: 197.1   Fiber: 1.3 g

Brazilian Green Beans

I first tasted this flavorful dish at the salad bar of a Brazilian steakhouse near my home. The next day I stocked up on green beans and set about duplicating the recipe. I added the sweet red pepper for a sprinkling of color.

Makes 7 servings

6 cups of snapped fresh green beans
1/2 cup mayonnaise
2 tsp Dijon-style mustard
1 tsp cider vinegar
1/4 tsp salt, or to taste
Dash white pepper
1/2 sweet red pepper, seeded and diced
2 Tbsp chopped chives or green onion tops

1. In a large saucepan or small pot, cook green beans to desired degree of doneness, 10 to 20 minutes. Cool under cold running water in a colander.
2. Meanwhile, in a large bowl, whisk together mayonnaise, mustard, vinegar, salt, and white pepper.
3. Stir in green beans, red pepper, and chives. Serve at once, or cover and refrigerate up to 24 hours. Stir before serving. Garnish with additional chopped red pepper and chives, if desired. The beans will keep in the refrigerator for 2 or 3 days.

Carbs: 9.1 g   Protein: 2.2 g   Calories: 155.5   Fiber: 3.6 g

Marinated Asparagus

The tangy dressing adds excellent flavor and texture to the asparagus.

Makes 4 servings

16 spears, 1/2-in diameter, fresh asparagus, well washed and
    coarse ends snapped off
1/4 cup olive oil
1 1/2 Tbsp tarragon vinegar
1/2 tsp celery salt
1/2 tsp Dijon-style mustard
1/8 tsp white pepper
Dash garlic powder
1 large hard-cooked egg finely chopped
1 Tbsp chopped fresh parsley

1. In a large saucepan over high heat, bring 3 inches of water
   to a boil. Add asparagus. Reduce heat and cook until just
   tender, about 5 minutes.
2. Meanwhile, in a medium bowl, whisk together oil, vinegar,
   celery salt, mustard, pepper, and garlic powder.
3. Transfer asparagus to a colander. Cool under running
   water. Drain. Arrange in a flat serving dish. Pour dressing
   over asparagus. Cover and refrigerate for 2 hours or up to
   24 hours. Before serving, garnish with chopped egg and
   parsley.

Carbs: 2.1 g   Protein: 3.4 g   Calories: 150.7 Fiber: 1.6 g

Roasted Asparagus

Roasting does wonderful things for asparagus.

Makes 4 servings

16 medium asparagus spears, well washed and coarse ends
      snapped off
1 Tbsp olive oil
1/8 tsp salt
1 1/2 Tbsp grated Parmesan cheese

1. Preheat the oven to 400 degrees. Dry the asparagus on
   paper towels. Place in a shallow roasting pan, spreading the
   spears out in 1 layer, if possible. Drizzle the spears with oil,
   and turn to coat. Sprinkle on salt.
2. Roast for 10 to 12 minutes or until the spears are tender.
   Remove to a serving dish, and sprinkle with Parmesan
   cheese.

Carbs: 1.8 g   Protein: 2.5 g   Calories: 50.1   Fiber: 1.6 g

Southern-style Green Beans
A quick and easy version of a southern classic.

4 bacon strips
2 14 1/2-oz cans green beans, including juice

1. In a small skillet, fry bacon strips over medium heat until crisp. When cool enough to handle, crumble or cut into 1-inch pieces.
2. In a saucepan, combine green beans and bacon. Bring to a boil. Reduce heat and simmer about 20 minutes until bacon flavors beans. Drain before serving.

Carbs: 6.9 g   Protein: 3.6 g   Calories: 70.6   Fiber: 3.4 g

Baked Cauliflower and Cheese

If you're craving macaroni and cheese, try this surprisingly good substitute. For mild flavor, use only the florets and small stem pieces.

Makes 5 servings

5 cups coarsely diced cauliflower florets.
2 Tbsp chopped onion
1 Tbsp butter
1/2 Tbsp white flour
3/4 cup heavy cream
1/8 tsp salt
Dash white pepper
2 cups grated Cheddar cheese

1. Butter a 9-inch deep dish pie plate or similar shallow casserole. Set aside. Preheat oven to 375 degrees.
2. In a large saucepan, combine cauliflower, onion, and 2 cups of water. Bring to a boil. Cover, reduce heat, and simmer 4 or 5 minutes until cauliflower is crisp-tender. Drain in a colander.
3. Meanwhile, in large saucepan over medium heat, melt the butter. Stir in the flour until well blended. Gradually pour in the cream, stirring until the mixture thickens, about 2 minutes. Remove from heat. Stir in salt, pepper, and cheese until cheese partially melts. Stir in cauliflower.

4. Transfer to pie plate, spreading mixture evenly. Bake uncovered for 20 minutes or until very bubbly and top just begins to brown.

Carbs: 7.7 g   Protein: 14.1 g   Calories: 356.1   Fiber: 2.6 g

Quick Parmesan Cauliflower

This fast and tasty casserole stands in very well for potatoes. I use small florets as is and cut larger ones in half or thirds.

Makes 5 servings

1/4 cup chicken broth
2 Tbsp melted butter
1/4 tsp celery salt
1/8 tsp white pepper
6 cups small cauliflower florets
1/4 cup grated Parmesan cheese

1. In a 1 1/2-quart microwave-safe casserole, combine broth, butter, celery salt, and pepper. Stir to mix well. Add cauliflower and stir to coat. Cover with casserole lid, and microwave on high power 8 to 10 minutes until cauliflower is cooked through, stopping and stirring once during microwaving.
2. Remove from microwave. Drain cauliflower in a colander. Return to casserole, and stir in Parmesan cheese.

Carbs: 6.5 g   Protein:4.2 g   Calories: 93   Fiber: 3 g

Portobello Slices

You'll love what balsamic vinegar and Parmesan do for these mushrooms.

Makes 3 servings

2 large portobello mushrooms, cut into 8 to 10 slices
3 Tbsp olive oil
Dash salt
1/8 tsp black pepper
2 tsp balsamic vinegar
1 Tbsp grated Parmesan cheese

1. In a large skillet, combine the mushrooms and oil. Sprinkle with salt and pepper.
2. Cook over medium heat 6 or 7 minutes or until the mushrooms have exuded their juices, softened, and begun to brown.
3. Remove the pan from the heat. Stir in the vinegar. Then toss to coat with cheese. Serve at once.

Carbs: 2 g   Protein: 1.4 g   Calories: 138.2   Fiber: 0.7 g

CHAPTER 3
Sensational Sauces, Dressings, and Butters

In this chapter, I've provided a nice selection of extras that will add flavor and texture to your meals. Here you'll find herb butters and rich sauces that enhance meat, fish, and vegetables. And for your salads, try Herb Dressing or Russian Dressing, both of which are far superior to anything you can buy in a bottle.

If you want Bearnaise Sauce, Parsley Onion Butter or Honey Mustard Sauce on your steak or cauliflower, there are easy-to-follow recipes here.

Pesto is another good choice to enliven meat or vegetables. And with a food processor, it's a snap to make.

Other traditional accompaniments you'll find are Cocktail Sauce, Horseradish Sauce, and a Louie Dressing that's wonderful on seafood or salad.

And one very useful addition to your repertory will be the homemade Barbecue Sauce. I've used it to make some wonderful pork ribs. It's equally good on chicken.

Basil-Parsley Pesto

There's nothing like the taste of fresh pesto. If you've enjoyed it in Italian restaurants, you may be surprised by how easy it is to make this topping at home. Serve over steak or sauteed zucchini or cauliflower. If you have a plentiful supply of fresh basil, you can increase the proportion of basil to parsley in the recipe.

Makes 6 servings, 1/4 Tbsp each

1/4 cup pine nuts
2 tsp chopped garlic
1 cup packed fresh basil leaves
1 cup packed fresh parsley leaves
1 Tbsp fresh lemon juice
1/2 tsp salt, or more to taste
1 cup olive oil
1 cup grated Parmesan cheese

1. Spread the pine nuts in a small, nonstick skillet. Cook over medium-high heat, stirring constantly with a wooden spoon, until the nuts begin to turn brown and smell toasted, about 3 or 4 minutes. Immediately transfer to a plate, and cool slightly.
2. Combine the nuts, garlic, basil, parsley, lemon juice, and salt in a food processor bowl. Process until finely minced. With the processor on, slowly pour in the oil through the feed tube; process until well blended, stopping and scraping down the sides of the container once or twice, if necessary.
3. Transfer to a medium bowl. Stir in cheese. Serve at room temperature, or cover and refrigerate. Pesto will keep tightly sealed in the refrigerator for up to a week. It can be frozen for longer storage.

Carbs: 2.9 g   Protein: 7.7 g   Calories: 423.5   Fiber: 0.9 g

Bearnaise Sauce

*This classic sauce must be made with care. But it's worth the effort.
Wonderful on steaks, it's equally good on cooked broccoli, cauliflower, or
asparagus. The secret of success is in following directions carefully and
having all the ingredients on hand before you start. I melt the butter in a
small glass bowl in the microwave for about 1 minute on high power. Be
careful not to let the water in the bottom of the double boiler boil or touch
the top pan. The sauce holds for several hours if kept in a warm place,
such as the middle of the stove top.*

Makes about 1 cup

3 large egg yolks
2 Tbsp heavy cream
1/4 tsp salt
Dash white pepper
2 Tbsp tarragon vinegar
1/2 cup butter, melted
Chopped parsley leaves, tarragon, or chives for garnish

1. In the top of a double boiler, whisk egg yolks, cream, salt,
   and pepper until thick. Set over hot, not boiling, water.
   Make sure bottom of double boiler does not touch water.
2. Add the vinegar gradually while whisking constantly. Cook,
   whisking constantly until sauce thickens, about 1 minute.
   Remove double boiler from heat, leaving top in place.
3. Whisking constantly, add butter, a tablespoon at a time,
   whisking vigorously after each addition.
4. Serve warm. Just before serving, stir, and garnish with
   chopped parsley, tarragon, or chives.

Carbs: 0.1 g   Protein: 0.4 g   Calories: 47.6   Fiber: 0 g

Roasted Onion Spread

If you love onions, one of the hard things about a lo-carb diet is limiting them. Here I've intensified their flavor by roasting, so you can use less. I serve this spread over hamburger and steak. By the way, you'll love the wonderful aroma wafting from your oven as the onions cook.

Makes a generous 16 servings, 1 Tbsp each

1/4 cup coarsely chopped onion
2 Tbsp olive oil
3/4 cup commercial sour cream
1/4 cup mayonnaise
1/2 tsp chopped garlic
1/4 tsp celery salt
2 or 3 drops hot pepper sauce

1. Preheat the oven to 375 degrees. In a small, shallow casserole, toss the onions with the oil.
2. Roast the onions, uncovered, in the upper half of the oven, stirring 2 or 3 times until they are very soft and beginning to brown, about 35 to 40 minutes. Remove the dish from the oven, and cool the onions slightly.
3. Mix together the sour cream, mayonnaise, garlic, celery salt, and hot pepper sauce. Stir in the onions and oil. Chill 2 or 3 hours to allow flavors to blend. Stir before serving. Leftovers will keep in the refrigerator 3 or 4 days.

Carbs: 0.6 g   Protein: 0.3 g   Calories: 60.1   Fiber: 0 g

Salad Dressings

I love the fresh taste of homemade salad dressings. Once you start making them yourself, you won't want to use the bottled variety. Since these dressings are both made the same way, I've grouped them together, with the directions at the end. Traditionally, dressings are shaken in a screw-top jar. I've found a plastic refrigerator container works just as well—if the lid fits tightly. Dressings may be kept in the refrigerator for about 10 days.

Russian Dressing

Some of my most vivid memories are of foods. When I was a small child, my family lived in an apartment on Connecticut Avenue in Washington, D. C. We used to walk up the street to a neighborhood restaurant where I loved the Russian dressing. This version recreates that childhood taste.

Makes 10 servings, 2 Tbsp each

1/4 cup cider vinegar
1/4 cup tomato sauce
2 Tbsp Splenda
1/2 tsp salt
1/4 tsp paprika
1/4 tsp dry mustard
1/4 tsp pepper
3/4 cup olive oil

Carbs: 1.2 g   Protein: 0.1 g   Calories: 147.2   Fiber: 0.1 g

Herb Dressing

I use this instead of bottled Italian Dressing.

Makes 8 servings, 2 Tbsp each

3/4 cup olive oil
2 1/2 Tbsp lemon juice
2 Tbsp red wine or cider vinegar
1 Tbsp water
1/2 tsp chopped garlic
1/2 tsp Dijon-style mustard
1/2 tsp salt, or more to taste
3/4 tsp dried thyme leaves
1/4 tsp dried oregano leaves
1/2 tsp Splenda
1/8 tsp white pepper

Carbs: 0.7 g   Protein: 0.1 g   Calories: 181.1   Fiber: 0.1 g

1. Combine all ingredients in a jar or plastic container with a tight fitting lid. Shake well. Use at once or refrigerate.

Oil and Vinegar Dressing with Blue Cheese

There's nothing wrong with creamy blue cheese dressing, but I like this variation, too. Because it tastes best fresh, I make it in small quantities.

Makes 4 generous 2-Tbsp servings

1/2 cup olive oil
1 Tbsp red wine vinegar
1/4 cup crumbled blue cheese

1. In a small bowl, combine oil and vinegar. Stir in blue cheese until about half the cheese is combined into the oil and vinegar mixture. Stir before serving. Dressing will keep in the refrigerator for about 10 days.

Carbs: 0.2 g   Protein: 1.5 g   Calories: 263   Fiber: 0 g

Louie Dressing

I fell in love with this tangy dressing years ago in San Francisco. It's wonderful with shrimp, crab, or lobster, or simply as a dressing for a green salad.

Makes 12 servings, 2 Tbsp each

1 cup mayonnaise
1/2 cup tomato sauce
1 Tbsp dill relish
2 tsp Splenda
2 tsp Dijon-style mustard
1/4 tsp celery salt

1. In a small bowl, combine mayonnaise, tomato sauce, dill relish, Splenda, mustard, and celery salt. Stir to mix well.
2. Cover and refrigerate thirty minutes or up to several hours before serving. Dressing will keep in the refrigerator for about 10 days.

Carbs: 0.9 g   Protein: 0.2 g   Calories: 137.9   Fiber: 0.2 g

Barbecue Sauce

This flavorful homemade barbecue sauce has become a mainstay in my kitchen. I love it on ribs and chicken. Incidentally, you may want to check brands of tomato sauce, as some have more carbs than others.

Makes 7 servings, 1/4 cup each

1 15-oz can tomato sauce
2 Tbsp Splenda
1/2 Tbsp cider vinegar
1/2 tsp chopped garlic
1/2 tsp dry mustard
1/4 tsp dried thyme leaves
1/8 tsp ground cloves
1/8 tsp black pepper

1. In a small bowl, mix all ingredients together. Use at once, or cover and refrigerate until needed. Mixture will keep in the refrigerator for up to 2 weeks

Carbs: 5 g   Protein: 0.9 g   Calories: 21.5   Fiber: 0.9 g

Flavored Butters

These butters add extra taste appeal when melted over meats, fish, poultry, or vegetables. For an elegant presentation, after the flavoring ingredients are added, roll the butter in wax paper to form a cylindrical shape. Chill. Then cut into slices as needed. Flavored butters will keep in the refrigerator for up to 2 weeks. Since these butters are all made the same way, I've grouped them together, with the directions at the end.

These recipes all make about 8 servings, 1 Tbsp each.

Parsley-Onion Butter

Great with beef—from steak to hamburgers.

1/4 lb butter, at room temperature
1 Tbsp chopped fresh parsley leaves
1 tsp instant minced onions
1 tsp lemon juice
1/8 tsp salt, or to taste

Carbs: 0.3 g   Protein: 0.2 g   Calories: 102.8   Fiber: 0 g

Tarragon Butter

Wonderful with poultry, fish, or meat.

1/4 lb butter, at room temperature
1 1/4 tsp dried tarragon leaves
1/4 tsp lemon juice
1/8 tsp salt, or to taste

Carbs: 0.1 g   Protein: 0.2 g   Calories: 102.6   Fiber: 0 g

Dill and Garlic Butter

Fresh dill makes this butter. Good with fish, poultry or meat.

1/4 lb butter, at room temperature
1 tsp chopped garlic
1 1/2 Tbsp chopped fresh dill weed
1 tsp lemon juice
1/8 tsp white pepper

Carbs: 0.2 g   Protein: 0.2 g   Calories: 102.6   Fiber: 0 g

Orange-Rosemary Butter

I love the combination of rosemary and orange extract in this butter which is excellent on grilled chicken.

1/4 lb butter, at room temperature
1 Tbsp Splenda
1 tsp dried rosemary, crumbled
1/2 tsp orange extract

Carbs: 0.4 g   Protein: 0.1 g   Calories: 103.9   Fiber: 0.1 g

1. In a small bowl, combine butter with flavoring ingredients. With a fork, mash and stir until well combined. Cover and refrigerate for thirty minutes or up to several hours before serving.

Cocktail Sauce

Perfect for dipping shrimp or lump crab meat.

Makes 16 servings, 1 Tbsp each

1 cup tomato sauce
1 tsp prepared white horseradish
2 tsp Splenda
1/2 tsp chili powder

1. In a small bowl, stir together tomato sauce, horseradish, Splenda, and chili powder. Cover and refrigerate at least 30 minutes and up to several hours before serving. Sauce will keep in the refrigerator for up to a week.

Carbs: 1.2 g   Protein: 0.2 g   Calories: 5.7   Fiber: 0.2 g

Horseradish and Cream

This traditional dressing is wonderful on prime ribs or steak.

Makes 15 servings, 1 Tbsp each

1/2 cup whipping cream
2 Tbsp prepared white horseradish
1/2 Tbsp water
1/8 tsp salt, or to taste

1. Place cream in a mixer bowl, and beat until whipped. Meanwhile, in a small bowl, stir together horseradish, water, and salt.
2. When cream is whipped, stir in horseradish mixture. Cover and refrigerate 20 to 30 minutes or several hours before serving. Sauce will keep in the refrigerator for 2 or 3 days.

Carbs: 0.3 g   Protein: 0.2 g   Calories: 31.6   Fiber: 0 g

Sweet and Sour Mustard Sauce

Excellent on steak, burgers, or ham.

Makes about 16 servings, 1 Tbsp each

1/2 cup mayonnaise
1/2 cup commercial sour cream
2 tsp Splenda
2 tsp cider vinegar
1 tsp dry mustard
2 tsp Dijon-style mustard
1/8 tsp salt
Dash white pepper

1. In a medium bowl, stir together mayonnaise and sour cream until well blended. Stir in Splenda, vinegar, mustards, salt, and pepper until well combined. Cover and refrigerate 30 minutes or up to several hours to allow flavors to blend. Sauce will keep in the refrigerator for up to a week.

Carbs: 0.4 g   Protein: 0.3 g   Calories: 64.7   Fiber: 0 g

CHAPTER 4
The Meat of the Matter
(As well as the chicken, eggs, and fish.)

Come home to all the old-fashioned favorites you love to eat but have probably skimped on in recent years because the conventional wisdom said that they were bad for you.

On a lo-carb eating plan, you can have T-bone steak every night; but when you get tired of grilled steak, try some of the tempting alternatives in this chapter. Beef Paprikash, Tangy Pot Roast with Vegetables, Barbecued Brisket, Philly Cheese Steak, Sloppy Joes, Italian Chicken with Peppers and Onions, Orange Roughy, Mediterranean-Style. You'll love these hearty, stick-to-the-ribs entrees.

This is also the chapter where I've included several egg and cheese dishes, some of which you can include in your breakfast menu. I'll show you the easy way to make main dish omelets, including a Pan Pizza Omelet. And also some wonderful quiches, such as Ham and Onion Quiche, Southwestern Quiche, and Salmon Quiche—rich and creamy entrees that were made for lo-carb eating.

Grilled Beef, Italian Style

Grilled meat is served as frequently in Italy as pizza and pasta. Here's a flavorful Italian-style marinaded steak.

Makes 3 or 4 servings

1 1/2 lb sirloin steak, cut 1-in thick
1/4 cup chopped onion
1/2 cup olive oil
1/2 cup red wine vinegar
1 Tbsp Italian seasoning
1/2 Tbsp Dijon-style mustard
2 tsp chopped garlic
1 tsp salt

1. Place steak in a zip-lock plastic food storage bag. In a small bowl, combine onion, oil, vinegar, Italian seasoning, mustard, garlic, and salt; and stir to mix well. Pour into bag with steak, distributing evenly over meat. Seal, arrange on a large plate, and refrigerate 6 to 8 hours or overnight.
2. Adjust rack 5 inches from broiler. Preheat broiler. Transfer meat to broiler pan. Broil meat for 11 to 18 minutes, turning once, until desired degree of doneness is reached.

Carbs: 2.8 g   Protein: 41.1 g   Calories: 591.9   Fiber: 0.5 g

Grilled Beef with Peppers

The Grilled Beef, Italian Style, above, tastes wonderful with grilled peppers. If you'd like to try the variation, follow the recipe below.

Makes 3 or 4 servings

1 recipe Grilled Beef, Italian Style (Page 68)
2 sweet medium peppers (green, and red, yellow, or orange),
   seeded and sliced
2 Tbsp olive oil

1. Make Grilled Beef, Italian Style.
2. While the meat is grilling, transfer 1/4 cup marinade to a
   large skillet. Add olive oil and peppers, and cook over
   medium high heat, stirring frequently, 7 or 8 minutes, until
   peppers begin to char. Serve peppers with beef.

Carbs: 7.9 g   Protein: 41.8 g   Calories: 692.7   Fiber: 2 g

Asian Steak

Here's a recipe I like to make on my George Foreman Grill, but you can do it in the broiler or on an outdoor grill.

Makes 2 servings

1/4 cup chicken broth
1/4 cup light soy sauce
1 tsp Splenda
1/2 tsp ground ginger
1 Tbsp sesame seeds
1 Tbsp Asian sesame oil
1/4 tsp hot pepper sauce
1 1/4 lb sirloin steak

1. In a flat, shallow baking dish, combine all marinade ingredients. Stir to mix well. Arrange steak in marinade. Spoon over some of the liquid.
2. Cover and refrigerate about 6 hours, turning steak occasionally.
3. Broil or grill to desired degree of doneness.

Carbs: 1 g   Protein: 52.1 g   Calories: 361.8   Fiber: 0.1 g

Beef Paprikash

Hearty and flavorful, this stew is wonderful on a cold winter night. For ease of preparation, I brown the beef cubes under the broiler, along with the onion and garlic.

Makes 5 servings

2 1/2 lb lean stew beef, cut into small bite-sized pieces
Salt and pepper to taste
1/2 cup chopped onion
1 tsp chopped garlic
1 8-oz can tomato sauce
1 1/2 cups chicken broth, divided
2 large celery stalks, sliced
1 Tbsp paprika
1 tsp dried thyme leaves
1 cup commercial sour cream

1. Preheat broiler. Arrange meat in a 9 1/2- by 13-inch baking pan. Adjust rack about 4 inches from heating element. Sprinkle with salt and pepper. Tuck onion and garlic among meat pieces. Broil 4 inches from heat about 12 to 15 minutes, stirring once or twice, until meat is browned.
2. Meanwhile, in a Dutch oven or similar large pot, combine tomato sauce and broth. Stir to mix well. Add celery. Stir in paprika and thyme.
3. Transfer the meat mixture to Dutch oven. Bring to a boil. Reduce heat, and simmer with the top ajar on the pot 1 to 1 1/2 hours or until the meat is tender and the sauce has cooked down slightly. Stir occasionally and check to make sure the sauce does not boil away. If sauce cooks down too much, reduce heat and add a bit of water.
5. Remove from heat. Stir in sour cream. Add salt and pepper to taste. Serve from pot.

Carbs: 8.2 g   Protein: 59.8 g   Calories: 462.5 Fiber: 1.6 g

Tangy Pot Roast with Vegetables

Here's a savory one-pot dinner. Leftovers can be quickly reheated in the microwave.

Makes 4 to 6 servings

1 2 1/2- to 3-lb chuck roast
Salt and pepper to taste
3 Tbsp olive oil
1 cup chicken broth
1/2 cup tomato sauce
1 Tbsp Splenda
1 Tbsp cider vinegar
1 1/2 tsp Dijon-style mustard
1 1/2 tsp dried thyme leaves
1 tsp chopped garlic
1 bay leaf
1/8 tsp black pepper
2 celery stalks, sliced
2 cups sliced cabbage
2 cups small cauliflower florets

1. Sprinkle roast with salt and pepper. In a large Dutch oven or similar pot over medium heat, brown meat in oil, turning to brown all sides. If the meat begins to stick to the bottom of the pot, reduce heat.
2. Add the broth. Scrape up any browned bits of meat from the pot bottom. Add the tomato sauce, Splenda, vinegar, mustard, thyme, garlic, bay leaf, and pepper. Stir to mix well. Stir in celery and cabbage, stirring them down into the sauce. Spoon some sauce over the meat. Bring to a boil. Cover the pot, reduce heat, and simmer about 2 to 2 1/2 hours, checking occasionally to make sure the sauce is not sticking to the bottom of the pot. If desired, with a flat spoon skim fat from surface of sauce and discard. Remove

meat to a plate, and keep warm. Add cauliflower. Uncover pot, raise heat, and cook down sauce until it reduces by about one half, about 8 to 10 minutes.

3. Remove and discard bay leaf. Slice roast and arrange on serving platter; surround with vegetables. Pour sauce over meat. Leftover roast will keep in the refrigerator for 3 or 4 days.

Carbs: 9.1 g   Protein: 69.8 g   Calories: 651.7   Fiber: 3.5 g

Barbecued Beef Brisket

If you've never cooked this cut of meat, you're in for a treat. There's nothing like a well-seasoned brisket roasted to perfection in the oven. Look for lean brisket, or trim off excess fat after cooking.

Makes 6 servings

3 lb well-trimmed beef brisket
1 tsp salt
1/4 tsp black pepper
1/2 cup chopped onion
1 cup water
1/3 cup tomato sauce
1/4 cup cider vinegar
1/4 cup Splenda
1 Tbsp Worcestershire sauce
1 tsp chopped garlic
1/8 tsp ground cloves
1 bay leaf

1. Preheat oven to 325 degrees. Arrange brisket in a 9 1/2- by 13-inch baking pan. Sprinkle with salt and pepper.
2. In a small bowl, combine onion, water, tomato sauce, vinegar, Splenda, Worcestershire sauce, garlic, and cloves. Pour over brisket. Tuck bay leaf into sauce in pan bottom.
3. Tightly cover with aluminum foil, and bake for about 3 1/2 to 4 hours until meat is tender.
4. Remove meat to a cutting board. With a sharp knife, cut meat across the grain into thin slices. Keep warm.

5. Meanwhile, place baking pan on stove burner, and cook down sauce over high heat, stirring frequently, until reduced by about half, 8 to 10 minutes. Return sliced meat to pan, and spoon sauce over top. Serve from pan, or transfer meat and sauce to a serving platter. Leftovers will keep in the refrigerator 3 or 4 days.

Carbs: 4.5 g   Protein: 34.9 g   Calories: 298   Fiber: 0.5 g

Sweet and Sour Ground Beef and Cabbage

This skillet dinner has the flavor of sweet and sour stuffed cabbage, with a fraction of the work. By the way, you should check labels on cans of tomato sauce, as some have more carbs than others.

Makes 2 servings

1 lb lean ground beef
1 tsp chopped garlic
1 cup thinly sliced cabbage
1/2 cup tomato sauce
1 Tbsp Splenda
1 Tbsp cider vinegar
1 tsp dried thyme leaves
1 bay leaf
Salt and pepper to taste

1. In a large skillet over medium heat, brown beef and garlic until beef is browned, about 5 or 6 minutes. Stir in sliced cabbage and tomato sauce. Stir in Splenda, vinegar, thyme, bay leaf, and salt and pepper to taste.
2. Bring to a boil. Reduce heat, cover, and simmer about 20 minutes until cabbage is almost tender and flavors are blended. Remove bay leaf. Serve in bowls.

Carbs: 8.6 g   Protein: 41.1 g   Calories: 480.1   Fiber: 2 g

Greek Lasagna

One interesting thing I discovered while traveling in Greece is that there's a lot of Italian influence in their cuisine. I decided to take this concept one step further and make a lasagna with Greek phyllo dough. The dough is so thin that it's very low in carbohydrates. Leftover dough can be used in other recipes or refrozen for later use.

Makes 8 servings

2 lb lean ground beef
1 cup chopped onion
1 tsp chopped garlic
1 15-oz can tomato sauce
1 tsp dried thyme leaves
1 tsp dried oregano leaves
1/2 tsp salt
Dash ground black pepper
1/4 cup melted butter
4 half phyllo sheets, thawed
1 8-oz package shredded mozzarella cheese, divided
1 cup ricotta cheese

1. Preheat oven to 350 degrees.
2. In a medium-sized pot over medium heat, cook ground beef, onion, and garlic until the beef is brown and the onions are soft.
3. Add tomato sauce, thyme, oregano, salt, and pepper. Bring to a boil. Reduce the heat, and simmer about 10 minutes, or until the flavors are partially blended.
4. Brush the bottom of a 9 1/2- by 13-inch pan with the melted butter. Unwrap the phyllo onto wax paper. Cover with additional wax paper and a barely damp tea towel. Working quickly, cut 4 large sheets in half at the folded edge, leaving them lying on the pile of dough sheets. Remove a half sheet, and lay it in the bottom of the pan.

77

Brush with melted butter.

5. Sprinkle 1/3 of the mozzarella cheese over the dough. Spoon half the beef filling on top, spreading the mixture evenly with the back of a large spoon or spatula. Add another phyllo layer and spread with butter.

6. In a medium bowl, mix 1 cup of the beef mixture with the ricotta cheese. Spoon the mixture onto the phyllo sheet, gently spreading it over the surface of the dough with the back of a large spoon. Add the remaining meat mixture. Sprinkle on 1/3 of the mozzarella cheese. Top with 2 phyllo half sheets, brushing each layer with the melted butter.

7. Bake for 35 to 40 minutes until top begins to brown. Sprinkle with the remaining mozzarella cheese during the last 6 minutes of baking. Let the lasagna stand for 5 minutes before cutting into 8 portions.

Carbs: 10.8 g   Protein: 31.9 g   Calories: 448.4   Fiber: 1.4 g

Stuffed Peppers, Greek-Style

Stuffed vegetables are one of the pleasures of Greek cooking. Here's a lo-carb version of one of my favorites, featuring 3 cheeses and spinach.

Makes 4 pepper halves

2 large green peppers, cut in half lengthwise, seeded, and
    stems removed
1 cup cut leaf frozen spinach
1 1/4 cups ricotta cheese
2 cups shredded mozzarella cheese
1/2 cup grated Parmesan cheese
1 Tbsp olive oil
1 tsp Italian seasoning
1 tsp chopped garlic
1/8 tsp ground nutmeg
Salt, to taste
2 or 3 drops hot pepper sauce

1. Parboil pepper halves for 2 or 3 minutes until partially cooked. Drain in a colander, and reserve in a baking dish. Preheat oven to 350 degrees.
2. Place the spinach in a small microwave-safe bowl, cover with wax paper, and microwave on 30 per cent power for 2 or 3 minutes, or until the spinach is thawed. Squeeze out excess moisture.
3. In a large bowl, stir together the ricotta, mozzarella, Parmesan, olive oil, Italian seasoning, garlic, nutmeg, salt, if desired, and hot pepper sauce. Stir in the spinach.

4. Mound cheese mixture into pepper halves, dividing evenly.
5. Bake for 25 to 30 minutes on the center oven rack or until the cheese is cooked through.

Carbs: 10.4 g   Protein: 28.7 g   Calories: 396.4   Fiber: 2.1 g

Lasagna Peppers

These stuffed peppers have the flavor of little mini-lasagnas—without those impossibly high-carb noodles.

Makes 6 pepper halves

3 large green peppers cut in half lengthwise, seeded, and stems
    removed
3/4 lb lean ground beef
1 cup Italian seasoned chunky tomato sauce, divided
1/3 cup ricotta cheese
3/4 cup shredded mozzarella cheese
1/4 cup grated Parmesan cheese

1. In a large pot, parboil pepper halves for 2 or 3 minutes until partially cooked. Drain in a colander, and reserve in a baking dish. Preheat oven to 350 degrees.
2. In a large skillet, cook the ground beef over medium heat, stirring frequently until browned, about 6 or 7 minutes. Stir in half the tomato sauce. Remove from heat. Divide the meat mixture evenly among the pepper halves.
3. Spoon the ricotta over the meat, dividing evenly. Sprinkle the mozzarella over the ricotta, dividing evenly. Top with the remaining tomato sauce, dividing evenly, then Parmesan, dividing evenly.
4. Bake for 25 to 30 minutes on the center oven rack or until the cheese is cooked through and the flavors are well blended.

Carbs: 11 g   Protein: 34.6 g   Calories: 416.8 Fiber: 2.8 g

Mexican Stuffed Peppers

If you crave Mexican food, here are stuffed peppers with south of the border flavor.

Makes 6 pepper halves

3 large green peppers, cut in half lengthwise, seeded, and
    stems removed
1 lb lean ground beef
1 cup mild salsa
1 tsp chili powder
1 cup shredded Cheddar cheese

1. Parboil pepper halves for 2 or 3 minutes until partially cooked. Drain in a colander, and reserve in a baking dish. Preheat oven to 350 degrees.
2. In a large skillet, cook the ground beef over medium heat, stirring frequently until beef is browned, about 6 or 7 minutes. Stir in the salsa and chili powder. Remove from heat.
3. Divide the meat mixture evenly among the pepper halves.
4. Bake for 20 to 25 minutes on the center oven rack or until the beef is bubbly. Top with the cheese, dividing evenly among the peppers. Cook an additional 3 or 4 minutes or until the cheese is melted.

Carbs: 10.2 g   Protein: 37.9   Calories: 487.6   Fiber: 2.9 g

Philly Cheese Steak

Fast food at its best! I love Philly Cheese steak, but I've always considered it much too decadent for frequent consumption. Now, with this breadless version, I can indulge whenever I want.

Makes 2 servings

1 lb very thinly sliced round steak, cut into slices
1 cup chopped onion
2 Tbsp olive oil
1 cup grated Cheddar cheese

1. In a large skillet over medium heat, cook the steak and onion in oil, stirring frequently, until steak is browned on all sides and onion is tender, about 5 or 6 minutes.
2. Sprinkle on the grated cheese. Cover with pan top, and cook an additional 1 or 2 minutes until cheese melts.

Carbs: 7.6 g   Protein: 65.9 g   Calories: 679   Fiber: 1.4 g

Sloppy Joes

One of my favorite quick dinners—updated for lo-carb cooking.

Makes 4 servings

2 lb lean ground beef
1/2 cup chopped onion
1 cup tomato sauce
2 Tbsp cider vinegar
2 Tbsp Splenda
1 tsp dried thyme leaves
1 large bay leaf
1/8 tsp ground cinnamon
1/8 tsp ground cloves
Salt and pepper to taste

1. In a Dutch oven or similar large, heavy pot, combine ground beef and onion. Cook over medium heat, stirring frequently, until beef is browned, about 6 or 7 minutes.
2. Add the tomato sauce, vinegar, Splenda, thyme, bay leaf, cinnamon, cloves, and salt and pepper to taste. Bring to a boil. Reduce heat, cover, and simmer 20 to 25 minutes until flavors are well blended. Remove bay leaf.

Carbs: 7.8 g   Protein: 40.9 g   Calories: 469.3   Fiber: 1.4 g

Barbecued Spare Ribs

Here's my favorite method for barbecuing ribs, which starts by boiling them in a large pot on the stove. By the time they reach the broiler or grill, they're already cooked through; and the spices in the water have added flavor to the meat.

Makes 2 or 3 servings

2 1/2 to 3 lb lean pork spare ribs
1 bay leaf
1 tsp whole cloves
1/4 tsp black pepper
3/4 to 1 cup homemade Barbecue Sauce (Page 61)

1. If necessary, cut rib rack in half. Place ribs in a large Dutch oven or similar pot. Cover with water. Add bay leaf, cloves, and pepper. Bring to a boil. Cover and reduce heat. Simmer 25 to 30 minutes.
2. Remove ribs from water. Dry with paper towels. Place in a baking pan. Brush top side with homemade barbecue sauce. Adjust rack about 4 inches from broiler. Broil 6 to 8 minutes, until ribs are crusty on the outside. Turn, brush with additional sauce, and broil an additional 6 to 8 minutes until crusty on outside. Or cook on the outdoor grill.

Carbs: 8.6 g   Protein: 65.4 g   Calories: 911.4   Fiber: 1.9 g

Pork Chops with Sauerkraut and Tomato

Caraway seeds give this pork and sauerkraut dinner a wonderful flavor.

Makes 2 servings

4 1/2-in-thick pork chops
1/8 tsp black pepper
2 or 3 Tbsp olive oil
1 8-oz can tomato sauce
1 cup canned sauerkraut, drained
1 1/2 tsp caraway seeds
1 tsp Splenda

1. Sprinkle pork chops with pepper. In a large skillet over medium heat, cook pork chops in oil until they change color, about 5 or 6 minutes.
2. Add the tomato sauce, sauerkraut, caraway seeds, and Splenda. Stir to mix well. Bring to a boil. Reduce heat, cover, and simmer about 20 minutes until pork chops are tender and flavors are well blended. Remove chops from pan and keep warm. Over medium-high heat, cook down the sauce, stirring occasionally, until reduced by half, 5 minutes. Serve sauce over chops.

Carbs: 11.3 g   Protein: 39.6 g   Calories: 447.6   Fiber: 3.6 g

Italian Chicken with Peppers and Onions

Here's an easy but delicious Italian chicken dinner. The dish goes together quickly because it features several convenience items: frozen pepper and onion stir fry, seasoned tomato sauce, and chopped garlic.

Makes 3 or 4 servings

3 Tbsp olive oil
1 tsp chopped garlic
1 1/2 lb boneless, skinless chicken breast meat, cut into large
    pieces
1 1/2 cups chunky, Italian-seasoned tomato sauce
2 cups frozen mixed pepper and onion stir-fry
Salt and pepper to taste
2 Tbsp grated Parmesan cheese

1. In a large, non-stick skillet, combine oil and garlic. Add the chicken; and cook over medium heat, stirring frequently, until chicken begins to brown, about 4 or 5 minutes.
2. Add the tomato sauce. Stir in pepper and onions. Bring to a boil. Reduce heat, cover, and simmer about 15 minutes. With a slotted spoon, remove chicken to a serving platter, and keep warm. Turn up heat under sauce. Bring to a boil; then cook uncovered, stirring occasionally until sauce is reduced by about half. Add salt and pepper to taste. Spoon sauce over chicken. Sprinkle Parmesan over all.

Carbs: 10.1 g   Protein: 54.3 g   Calories: 450.9 Fiber: 3.5 g

Greek-Style Chicken

This easy chicken dish combines some classic flavors from Greek cuisine. Cutting the chicken into bite-sized pieces shortens the cooking time considerably. Pitted olives are preferable, but unpitted will also work.

Makes 3 servings

3 Tbsp olive oil
1 1/2 lb boneless, skinless chicken breast, cut into bite-sized
  pieces
1/2 chopped green pepper
1 tsp chopped garlic
1/2 cup tomato sauce
1/3 cup chicken broth
1/2 cup oil-cured black olives, drained
1 tsp dried thyme leaves
1/2 cup crumbled feta cheese

1. In a large skillet, combine oil, chicken, pepper, and garlic.
   Cook over medium heat, stirring frequently, until chicken is
   white on all sides, about 8 minutes
2. Add tomato sauce, broth, olives, and thyme. Bring to a boil,
   reduce heat, cover, and simmer, stirring occasionally, about
   10 minutes until chicken is almost tender. Stir in feta
   cheese. Uncover, raise heat, and cook an additional 5
   minutes, until flavors have blended and sauce has
   thickened slightly.

Carbs: 8 g   Protein: 54.4 g   Calories: 498.7   Fiber: 1.4 g

Kung Pao Chicken

When I first started lo-carb cooking, I was worried that I'd have to give up Chinese food. But it turned out that all I had to do was alter classic recipes slightly. Here's one of my all-time favorites. The crunchy peanuts make a wonderful contrast to the chicken.

Makes 2 or 3 servings

Marinade
2 tsp rice or white vinegar
2 Tbsp soy sauce
5 to 8 drops hot oil or hot pepper sauce, or to taste (optional)
1 Tbsp finely chopped fresh ginger or 1 tsp ground ginger
1 green onion, sliced
Chicken and Vegetables
1 lb boneless, skinless chicken breast, cut into bite-sized
   pieces
1/3 cup salted peanuts
1/3 cup peanut oil, or more if needed
1/2 cup tender broccoli stalks, diced
3/4 cup thinly sliced cabbage
Seasonings
1 Tbsp soy sauce
2 tsp Splenda
1 tsp rice or white vinegar

1. Mix vinegar, soy sauce, hot oil, ginger, and onion in a large, non-reactive bowl. Stir in chicken. Marinate 15 minutes at room temperature (or up to 12 hours if refrigerated).
2. Meanwhile, combine peanuts and oil in a large skillet or wok. Over medium high heat, cook peanuts until they begin to brown, stirring, about 3 or 4 minutes. Remove peanuts with a slotted spoon, and reserve in a small bowl. In skillet over medium-high heat, cook broccoli stalks and cabbage in oil until crisp-tender, stirring, about 3 or 4

minutes. With a slotted spoon, transfer vegetables to bowl with peanuts.

3. Add marinated chicken and marinade to skillet. Add additional oil if needed. Cook chicken over medium high heat, stirring, until it changes color, about 3 minutes. Add soy sauce, Splenda, and vinegar, along with reserved peanuts and vegetables. Cook, stirring, an additional 3 or 4 minutes until chicken is cooked through.

Carbs: 10.6 g   Protein: 59.2 g   Calories: 757.3   Fiber: 3.6 g

Orange Roughy, Mediterranean-Style

This fast and flavorful fish dinner features orange roughy, but you can substitute any mild white fish such as flounder.

Makes 2 servings

1/2 cup chicken broth
1/4 cup olive oil, divided
1/2 large green pepper, seeded and chopped
1/4 cup chopped onion
2 Tbsp chopped oil-packed sun-dried tomatoes
1 tsp chopped garlic
1 tsp dried basil leaves
1 lb fresh or frozen (thawed) fillets of orange roughy
Salt and pepper to taste
1 1/2 Tbsp grated Parmesan cheese

1. In a small saucepan, combine broth, 2 tablespoon oil, pepper, onion, tomatoes, garlic, and basil. Stir to mix well. Bring to a boil. Reduce heat, and cook, uncovered, over medium heat 6 to 8 minutes, stirring frequently, until onions are very tender, and sauce has cooked down somewhat. Keep warm over low heat, stirring occasionally.
2. Meanwhile, sprinkle fish with salt and pepper. In batches, if necessary, cook fish in remaining oil in a large skillet over medium heat until cooked through, about 2 to 5 minutes per side, depending on thickness.
3. Arrange fish on a serving platter. Arrange vegetable mixture over fish. Sprinkle Parmesan over all.

Carbs: 5.8 g   Protein: 35.1 g   Calories: 445.3 Fiber: 1.4 g

Grilled Fresh Salmon with Dill

I like to make this simple but tasty entree with salmon fillets. If only salmon steaks are available, you will need to coat them with a bit more oil when they are turned. Dill goes beautifully with broiled salmon. But you could also substitute thyme and basil.

Makes 2 servings

Marinade
2 Tbsp olive oil
3/4 tsp chopped fresh dill leaves or generous 1/4 tsp dried
    dill weed
1/2 tsp lemon juice
1/8 tsp salt
1/8 tsp black pepper

Fish
1 lb boneless salmon fillet
Fresh dill sprigs, for garnish (optional)

1. In a cup, combine oil, dill, lemon juice, salt, and pepper. Stir to combine.
2. Place fillets skin side down on an oiled broiler pan. With a teaspoon, drizzle the marinade over the fish, and spread it evenly with the back of the spoon. Allow the fish to marinate about 8 to 10 minutes at room temperature.
3. Broil the fish in a preheated broiler about 5 inches from the heat. Broil 6 to 10 minutes per side, depending on the thickness of the fish, or until the flesh has turned pink and flakes easily with a fork. When turning the fillet, use a broad spatula under the thickest part; and turn it gently.
4. If desired, remove and discard fish skin. Turn individual portions dill-side up. Garnish with a sprig of fresh dill.

Carbs: 0.1 g   Protein: 43.3 g   Calories: 349.3 Fiber: 0 g

Shrimp with Olives and Feta Cheese

The feta cheese and olives give this quick and easy shrimp skillet a wonderful flavor.

Makes 2 servings

1 cup chunky Italian seasoned tomato sauce
1 lb ready-to-cook or cooked shrimp
12 large green pimiento olives, sliced
1/2 cup crumbled Feta cheese

1. In a large skillet, combine the tomato sauce, shrimp, and olives. Cook over medium heat, stirring frequently, until shrimp is heated through, about 3 or 4 minutes.
2. Stir in cheese, and simmer an additional 1 or 2 minutes.

Carbs: 8.7 g   Protein: 53.3 g   Calories: 365.6   Fiber: 2.2 g

Creamy Tuna over Broccoli

Here's what I make when I get a yen for tuna casserole.

Makes 2 or 3 servings

2 Tbsp butter
1 Tbsp white flour
3/4 cup heavy cream
1/4 cup water
2 6 1/2-oz cans water-packed tuna, drained and flaked
1/2 Tbsp instant minced onions
1/2 tsp dried basil leaves
Generous 1/4 tsp celery salt
Dash garlic powder
1/8 tsp salt, or to taste
Dash white pepper, or to taste
2 cups small broccoli florets,

1. In a medium saucepan, melt butter over medium heat. Stir in flour until well blended. Mix together cream and water. Gradually pour cream mixture into butter mixture, stirring until the sauce thickens.
2. Stir in the tuna, onions, basil, celery salt, garlic powder, and salt and pepper to taste. Reduce heat to low, cover, and keep mixture warm, stirring occasionally.
3. Meanwhile, place broccoli in a 4-cup measure or similar medium bowl. Add 1/4 cup water. Cover with wax paper, and microwave 4 or 5 minutes until broccoli is tender; or quickly steam broccoli in a saucepan. Drain broccoli in a colander. Serve tuna over broccoli.

Carbs: 11.3 g   Protein: 52.2 g   Calories: 673.1   Fiber: 3 g

Salmon Pie

I'm a fan of salmon—both because I love the taste and because I know it's so nutritious. This recipe is a lot like my old favorite salmon loaf, only it's quicker and easier.

Makes 3 or 4 servings

2 14 1/2-oz cans of pink salmon, drained and skin removed
1 large egg
1/2 cup mayonnaise
2 large celery stalks, diced
1 1/2 Tbsp instant minced onions
1 tsp Worcestershire sauce
1 tsp dry mustard
1/8 tsp celery salt
Dash white pepper
1 Tbsp chopped fresh parsley leaves for garnish (optional)

1. Preheat oven to 350 degrees. Butter the bottom and sides of a 9 inch pie plate. Set aside.
2. Place salmon in a large bowl, and use a fork to flake it. Add the egg, mayonnaise, celery, onion, Worcestershire sauce, mustard, celery salt, and pepper. Stir to mix well.
3. Spread evenly in prepared pie plate. Bake for 25 to 30 minutes or until top begins to brown.
4. Garnish with chopped parsley, if desired. Cut into wedges and serve.

Carbs: 3.7 g   Protein: 58.8 g   Calories: 728.4   Fiber: 0.7 g

Bacon and Cheese Omelet

I used to think that making omelets was difficult, until I developed this easy method. This omelet makes a nice brunch or luncheon entree.

Makes 2 servings

3 or 4 bacon strips, cut into 2-in pieces
1/4 cup chopped green pepper
2 Tbsp chopped onion
5 large eggs
Salt to taste
1/8 tsp black pepper
1/2 cup shredded Cheddar cheese

1. In a large non-stick skillet with sloping sides, combine bacon, green pepper, and onion. Cook over medium heat, stirring frequently, until bacon is almost crisp, about 5 or 6 minutes.
2. Meanwhile, place the eggs in a medium bowl. With a fork, beat in the salt and pepper.
3. When bacon is almost crisp, add the eggs to the pan, tipping the pan so that the egg mixture covers the entire bottom. Cook over medium heat for 2 minutes. Sprinkle cheese over top of the egg mixture. Cover and cook an additional 3 or 4 minutes or until eggs are set.
4. With a plastic spatula, cut the omelet into 2 servings. Fold each, and transfer the servings to individual plates.

Carbs: 4.7 g   Protein: 25.9 g   Calories: 366.2   Fiber: 0.7 g

Broccoli-Cheese Omelet

Here's another easy omelet with the richness of Cheddar cheese and the crunch of broccoli florets.

Makes 2 servings

3 Tbsp olive oil
1 cup finely chopped broccoli florets
2 Tbsp chopped onion
5 large eggs
1/2 tsp dried basil leaves
Salt to taste
1/8 tsp black pepper
1 cup shredded Cheddar cheese

1. In a large non-stick skillet with sloping sides, combine oil, broccoli, and onion. Cook over medium heat, stirring frequently, until the onion is tender, about 5 or 6 minutes.
2. Meanwhile, place eggs in a medium bowl. With a fork, beat in basil, salt, and pepper.
3. When onion is tender, add eggs to pan, tipping the pan so that the egg mixture covers the entire bottom. Cook over medium heat for 2 minutes. Sprinkle cheese over the top of the egg mixture. Cover and cook an additional 3 or 4 minutes or until the eggs are set.
4. With a plastic spatula, cut the omelet into 2 servings. Fold each and transfer the servings to individual plates.

Carbs: 5.7 g   Protein: 31.2 g   Calories: 609.6   Fiber: 1.7 g

Pan Pizza Omelet

Here's one of my favorite pizza making techniques. You get the great flavor of pizza on a carb-free omelet base.

Makes 2 servings

1 Tbsp butter
4 large eggs
Salt and pepper to taste
15 pepperoni slices
1/2 cup chunky Italian-flavored tomato sauce
1 cup shredded mozzarella cheese
2 Tbsp grated Parmesan cheese

1. In a large nonstick skillet, melt butter over medium heat. Meanwhile, in a small bowl, beat eggs, and add salt and pepper to taste. When butter is melted, pour eggs into pan, and tip so that the entire bottom surface is covered. Arrange the pepperoni over the surface of the eggs. Cover and cook about 3 minutes or until the eggs have set and begun to fluff.
2. Reduce heat to medium low. Spoon dollops of tomato sauce over egg surface. Lightly spread out tomato sauce with spoon back. Sprinkle with mozzarella, then Parmesan cheese. Cover and cook an additional 2 or 3 minutes or until mozzarella melts.
3. Uncover. With a wide rubber spatula, carefully loosen omelet. Using the side of the spatula, cut the omelet into 4 pizza "slices." Transfer slices to individual plates. Eat with a fork.

Carbs: 6.6 g   Protein: 32.5 g   Calories: 470.7   Fiber: 1.1 g

Ham and Onion Quiche

Easy as pie! Creamy and satisfying. Quiche is the perfect food for a lo-carb diet, which is why I've included several in this book. It makes a great company breakfast or luncheon entree. And it's not a bad dinner either. Swiss cheese is the usual choice for quiche, but you can make it with Mozzarella if that's what you have on hand.

Makes 3 or 4 servings

5 large eggs
3/4 cup heavy cream
1/8 tsp salt
1/8 tsp white pepper
3/4 cup shredded Swiss or Mozzarella cheese
1 cup diced ham
2 Tbsp finely chopped onion

1. Butter a 9-inch pie plate. Set aside. Preheat oven to 350 degrees.
2. In a medium bowl, beat eggs with a fork. Beat in cream and salt and pepper. Stir in cheese, ham, and onion. Pour into prepared pie plate.
3. Bake for 32 to 38 minutes, or until the quiche is browned around the edges of the top, and a knife inserted in the center comes out clean. Cool slightly before serving.

Carbs: 3.3 g   Protein: 31.4 g   Calories: 515.6   Fiber: 0.1 g

Broccoli-Cheddar Quiche

Here's a tasty twist on the quiche theme.

Makes 3 or 4 servings

1 1/2 cups chopped broccoli florets
2 Tbsp chopped onion
5 large eggs
1 cup heavy cream
1/2 tsp dried basil leaves
1/8 tsp salt
1/8 tsp white pepper
1 cup shredded Cheddar Cheese

1. Butter a 9-inch pie plate. Set aside. Preheat oven to 350 degrees.
2. In a 2-cup measure or similar small bowl, combine broccoli and onion. Add 2 tablespoons of water. Cover and microwave on high power 2 minutes. Drain well in a sieve or colander.
3. Meanwhile, in a medium bowl, beat eggs with a fork. Beat in cream, basil, salt, and pepper. Stir in cheese, broccoli, and onion. Pour into prepared pie plate.
4. Bake for 32 to 38 minutes, or until quiche is browned around the edges of the top, and a knife inserted in the center comes out clean. Cool slightly before serving.

Carbs: 6.8 g   Protein: 22.8 g   Calories: 565.2   Fiber: 1.6 g

Southwestern Quiche

Since quiche is so perfect for the lo-carb way of eating, I've provided another easy variation—with southwestern flavor. The ingredients are all staples in my kitchen, including the green chili. After opening, leftovers can be stored in a plastic container in the refrigerator for up to a week.

Makes 3 or 4 servings

5 large eggs
1 cup heavy cream
1/2 tsp chili powder
1/8 tsp salt
1 cup shredded Cheddar cheese
1/3 cup canned chopped chili peppers
1 tsp chopped garlic

1. Butter a 9-inch pie plate. Set aside. Preheat oven to 350 degrees.
2. In a medium bowl, beat eggs with a fork. Beat in cream, chili powder, and salt. Stir in cheese, peppers, and garlic. Pour into prepared pie plate.
3. Bake for 32 to 38 minutes, or until quiche is browned around the edges of the top, and a knife inserted in the center comes out clean. Cool slightly before serving.

Carbs: 5.1 g   Protein: 21.7 g   Calories: 555.5   Fiber: 0.4 g

Salmon Quiche

Yet another good and easy quiche, made with ingredients I always have on hand.

Makes 3 or 4 servings

1 6-oz can skinless, boneless salmon
5 large eggs
3/4 cup heavy cream
3/4 cup shredded Swiss cheese
1 tsp instant minced onions
1 tsp dried dill weed
1/8 tsp salt
Dash white pepper

1. Butter a 9-inch pie plate. Set aside. Preheat oven to 350 degrees.
2. Drain salmon and flake with a fork. Reserve in a small bowl.
3. In a medium bowl, beat eggs with a fork. Beat in cream. Stir in cheese, reserved salmon, onions, dill, salt, and pepper. Pour into prepared pie plate.
4. Bake for 32 to 38 minutes, or until quiche is browned around the edges, and a knife inserted in the center of comes out clean. Cool slightly before serving.

Carbs: 3.2 g   Protein: 30.5 g   Calories: 518.7   Fiber: 0.1 g

CHAPTER 5
Dazzling Desserts

Wonderful desserts without sugar and flour?

You bet. In this chapter you'll find Pecan Cake, Chocolate Hazelnut Cookies, Key Lime Pie, Fruit Pizza with Marzipan Crust, and Strawberry Mousse, all made without either sugar or flour.

The sweetener I prefer in my desserts is Splenda, the wonderful new product developed by the Johnson and Johnson company. It's made from sugar, so it beats all the other sweeteners for taste appeal. Although it doesn't behave exactly like sugar in *every* situation, it's close enough so that it can be used in many different situations.

Other ingredients I've come to rely on are whipping cream, cream cheese, gelatin, and ground nuts, which stand in so well for flour in baked goods.

There's something here for every sweet tooth. If you crave candy, try my delicious Marzipan or Chocolate Hazelnut Truffles.

If a big bowl of ice cream is your idea of heaven, I've provided several recipes, including Coffee Ice Cream and Strawberry Ice Cream. Making them is a snap with the new ice cream machines that require no messy ice and salt. You simply freeze the container in the freezer, then take it out and pour in the ingredients.

And if you want to finish off an elegant dinner in style, try my Almond Cream Cheese Tarts or the Strawberry Tarts, made in crisp little phyllo dough shells. Phyllo, used for making Greek pastries, is so thin that it's astonishingly low in carbs.

Marzipan Candy

My husband's favorite candy happens to be marzipan. So I was thrilled when I figured out how to make it for him. It's easy and delicious. Just be sure to use yolks from pasteurized eggs, and store tightly wrapped in the refrigerator.

Makes 30 servings

1 6-oz package blanched, slivered almonds.
1 cup Splenda
2 large pasteurized egg yolks
2 tsp almond extract
1 tsp lemon juice.

1. In food processor bowl, process almonds until very finely ground. Turn off machine, and add Splenda, egg yolks, almond extract, and lemon juice. Process until mixture forms a ball, or is well combined.
2. On a piece of wax paper, roll marzipan into a 10-inch cylindrical shape. Cut off pieces of candy as desired. Alternatively, you can add a few drops of food coloring and roll portions into fruit shapes. Store tightly wrapped in refrigerator. Marzipan will keep for up to 10 days.

Carbs: 2 g   Protein: 1.4 g   Calories: 44.9   Fiber: 0.6 g

Orange Almond Candy

Another candy made with ground almonds and pasteurized egg yolks

Makes 30 servings

1 6-oz package blanched, slivered almonds
1 cup Splenda
2 large pasteurized egg yolks
1 1/4 tsp orange extract
1 tsp water

1. In food processor bowl, process almonds until very finely
   ground. Turn off machine, and add Splenda, egg yolks,
   orange extract, and water. Process until mixture forms a
   ball or is well combined. If desired, add a few drops of
   orange food coloring.
2. On a piece of wax paper, roll mixture into a 10-inch
   cylindrical shape. Cut off pieces of candy as desired. Store
   tightly wrapped in refrigerator. Candy will keep for up to a
   week.

Carbs: 2 g   Protein: 1.4 g   Calories: 44.5   Fiber: 0.6 g

Almond Coconut Candy

One more candy flavor.

Makes 30 servings

1 6-oz package blanched, slivered almonds
1 cup Splenda
2 large pasteurized egg yolks
2 tsp imitation coconut flavoring
1 tsp water

1. In food processor bowl, process almonds until very finely ground. Turn off machine, and add Splenda, egg yolks, coconut flavoring, and water. Process until mixture forms a ball or is well combined
2. On a piece of wax paper, roll mixture into a 10-inch cylindrical shape. Cut off pieces of candy as desired. Store tightly wrapped in refrigerator. Candy will keep for up to a week.

Carbs: 2 g   Protein: 1.4 g   Calories: 44.8   Fiber: 0.6 g

Marzipan, Orange, or Coconut Truffles

I make these easy candy truffles using the almond candy recipes above.

For each truffle, roll a small piece of marzipan, orange almond candy, or coconut almond candy into a 3/4-inch ball. Roll in cocoa powder until coated, using a scant 1/4 teaspoon cocoa powder for each ball.

Carbs: 2.1 g   Protein: 1.4 g   Calories: 45.5   Fiber: 0.6 g

Hazelnut Truffles

These sweet treats are made with pasteurized egg white.

Makes 10 to 12 servings

1 cup ground hazelnuts
1 pasteurized egg white
1/2 cup Splenda
1/2 tsp vanilla extract
2 1/2 tsp cocoa powder

1. In a food processor container, combine hazelnuts, egg white, Splenda, vanilla. Process until mixture forms a ball.
2. One at a time, roll hazelnut mixture into 3/4-inch balls. Spread cocoa powder on a large plate. Roll each ball in cocoa powder. Store tightly covered in refrigerator. Candies will keep for up to 10 days.

Carbs: 4 g   Protein: 2 g   Calories: 103.6   Fiber: 1.2 g

Almond Macaroons

Sweet and crunchy, these almond cookies are a snap to make. Since they have no flour, they are very low in carbs. I recommend using a stand mixer, since it does take a bit of time to whip the egg whites. I grind the almonds in a food processor.

Makes about 24 cookies

3 egg whites
1/8 tsp salt
3/4 cup Splenda
1 1/2 cups ground blanched almonds (6 oz)
1/2 tsp almond extract

1. Heat oven to 350 degrees. Butter a large cookie sheet.
2. In an absolutely fat-free mixer bowl, beat egg whites and salt until frothy. Gradually add Splenda, beating continuously until mixture forms peaks that hold their shape, stopping and scraping down sides of bowl once. Then by hand, fold in almonds and almond extract.
3. Drop by walnut-sized spoonfuls of batter onto cookie sheet, spacing cookies about 2 inches apart. Bake in center of oven for 12 to 14 minutes or until lightly browned. Store in a closed container. Cookies will keep for 3 or 4 days.

Carbs: 2.3 g   Protein: 2.2 g   Calories: 42.7   Fiber: 0.6 g

Chocolate Hazelnut Cookies.

The combination of cocoa powder and hazelnuts gives these flourless cookies a great flavor.

Makes about 21 cookies

3 egg whites
1/8 tsp salt
1 1/4 cups Splenda
1 1/2 cups ground hazelnuts (6 oz)
3 Tbsp cocoa powder
1 tsp vanilla extract

1. Heat oven to 325 degrees. Butter a large cookie sheet.
2. In an absolutely fat-free mixer bowl, beat egg whites and salt until frothy. Gradually add Splenda, beating continuously until mixture will form peaks that hold their shape.
3. Meanwhile, in a large bowl, stir together nuts and cocoa. By hand, fold into egg whites, adding 1/2 of mixture at a time. Fold in vanilla extract.
4. Drop by small walnut-sized portions onto cookie sheet, spacing cookies about 2 inches apart. Bake in center of oven for 17 to 19 minutes or until lightly browned. Store in a closed container. Cookies will keep 3 or 4 days.

Carbs: 3.2 g   Protein: 1.4 g   Calories: 63.2   Fiber: 0.7 g

Peanut Cookies

These cookies have the great taste of fresh peanuts. I chop the peanuts in a food processor, until they are reduced to eighth-inch or slightly smaller pieces, just enough so the cookies have some crunch.

Makes about 26 cookies

3 egg whites
3/4 cup Splenda
2 cups coarsely chopped dry roasted peanuts (10 oz)
1 tsp vanilla extract

1. Heat oven to 350 degrees. Butter a large cookie sheet.
2. In an absolutely fat-free mixer bowl, beat egg whites until frothy. Gradually add Splenda, beating continuously until mixture forms peaks that hold their shape. By hand, fold in peanuts and vanilla extract.
3. Drop by walnut-sized portions onto cookie sheet. Bake in center of oven for 12 to 14 minutes or until firm and browned. Remove to racks. Store in a closed container. Cookies will keep 3 or 4 days at room temperature.

Carbs: 3.2 g   Protein: 3.1 g   Calories: 70.8   Fiber: 0.9 g

Toffee-Flavored Pecans

A handful of nuts makes a great snack. A handful of sweetened buttery nuts makes a quick and easy dessert. In creating this recipe, I've used English Toffee-flavored sugar free syrup from the Da Vinci Gourmet company. For an easy variation on this recipe, substitute one of their other syrups, such as Caramel or Coconut. Buying information for the syrups is on Page 136.

Makes 8 servings

2 Tbsp butter
1 cup pecan halves
1 1/2 Tbsp Da Vinci Gourmet English Toffee-flavored sugar free syrup

1. In a small skillet, melt butter over medium heat. Add nuts and saute, stirring, about 3 or 4 minutes until nuts begin to brown. Pour in syrup. Saute an additional minute. Turn out nuts onto a paper-towel covered plate. Cool. Leftover nuts will keep in the refrigerator for up to a week.

Carbs: 2 g   Protein: 1.5 g   Calories: 121.9   Fiber: 1.5 g

Pecan Crust

Of course when you're fixing dessert just for the family, you can make any pie without a crust. But when you're serving a company meal, this crust adds a finishing touch. I particularly like to use the recipe with the Key Lime Pie on Page 115 and the Mocha Pie on Page 116. For a thin, even crust, the pecans should be finely ground in the food processor until they begin to stick together.

Makes 1 9- or 10-inch pie crust (9 or 10 servings)

1 1/4 cups finely ground pecans
2 Tbsp Splenda
1/4 cup melted butter

1. Heat oven to 400 degrees.
2. In a small bowl, mix together pecans, Splenda, and butter. Moisten fingers with water, and press mixture firmly against bottom and sides of a 9-inch pie plate. Press a base of crust into the flat portion of the plate. Then work some of the mixture up the sides of the plate. Finally, return to the middle, and smooth out the crust into a thin layer. If crust sticks to fingers, moisten them again. Bake until lightly browned, about 6 to 8 minutes. Cool.

Carbs: 2.6 g   Protein: 1.7 g   Calories: 154.7   Fiber: 1.7 g

Marzipan Crust

Here's a fantastic crust you can use for many desserts, including the Fruit Pizza on Page 114. If making a crust, use a 9-inch pie plate. If making a fruit pizza, use a 10-inch pie plate.

Makes 9 servings

1 6-oz package blanched, slivered almonds.
1/3 cup Splenda
1/4 cup warm water.
1 tsp almond extract
2 large egg whites

1. In food processor, process almonds until very finely ground.
2. In a 4-cup measure or similar medium bowl, combine Splenda and water. Stir in almond extract. Add egg whites.
3. Add ground almonds, and work the mixture into a paste with your hands. Transfer to a 9- or 10-inch pie plate, and pat into a circle with a slight raised area at the edge. Cover with wax paper, and microwave on high power about 2 minutes or until almond paste is somewhat firm. If crust has risen from center of plate, press it back into place. If using for a pie crust, cool slightly and use fingers to press some crust from the flat area at the bottom up the sides of the pie plate. If using for Fruit Pizza, do not alter crust shape. Continue to microwave, covered with wax paper, in 30-second increments, until crust is almost dry in center—about 1 to 2 more minutes.
4. Cool crust and use as a pie base or for Fruit Pizza, Page 114.

Carbs: 4.8 g   Protein: 4.8 g   Calories: 131.6   Fiber: 2 g

Fruit Pizza

Here's a truly wonderful, colorful dessert that always garners rave reviews. I've made it with very lo-carb fruit. You could also use some raspberries or blackberries if you like.

Makes 9 servings

1 recipe Marzipan Crust (Page 113)
3 oz cream cheese at room temperature
2 Tbsp heavy cream
1 Tbsp Splenda
3/4 cup thinly sliced strawberries
1 kiwi fruit, peeled and cut into thin circles

1. Make Marzipan Crust. Set aside to cool.
2. In a small bowl, heat cream cheese in microwave for 20 seconds at high power. Combine cream cheese, cream, and Splenda; and whisk until uniform. Spoon dollops of cream cheese mixture onto crust. Spread in a uniform layer using the back of a tablespoon.
3. Attractively arrange sliced fruit over cream cheese mixture. Refrigerate. When cool, cover with plastic wrap. Or serve pizza immediately. The pizza can be made up to 12 hours before serving. It will keep in the refrigerator for 2 or 3 days, but the cream cheese layer may start to absorb color from the fruit after 24 hours.

Carbs: 7.4 g   Protein: 5.7 g   Calories: 185.5   Fiber: 2.6 g

Key Lime Pie

Key Lime Pie is one of my favorite desserts, so making a lo-carb version was one of my goals in writing this book. The results are fantastic, if I do say so myself. Although I don't usually use milk in lo-carb recipes, the evaporated milk contributes significantly to the flavor. You can make this pie without a crust, if you like. I purchase my key lime juice at a gourmet shop in my area. If you can't find the juice near home, buying information is on Page 136.

Makes 9 servings

1 9-inch Pecan Crust, if desired (Page 112)
1 envelope unflavored gelatin
1/2 cup cold water
4 large egg yolks
1/2 cup evaporated milk
1/2 cup Splenda
1/3 cup key lime juice
1/8 tsp salt
1 cup whipping cream

1. In a custard cup, soften gelatin in cold water. Set aside.
2. In a mixer bowl, beat egg yolks until light and lemon colored, about 4 or 5 minutes.
3. In the top of a double boiler, mix milk, Splenda, lime juice, salt, and egg yolks. Cook over boiling water, stirring constantly with a wooden spoon, until mixture thickens, about 5 minutes. Stir in gelatin until dissolved. Refrigerate to cool slightly.
4. In a large mixer bowl, whip cream until stiff. Fold in lime mixture. Spoon into pie shell or pie plate. Refrigerate at least 3 hours. Garnish with twists of lime, if desired.

Carbs: 7.7 g   Protein: 4.6 g   Calories: 301.6   Fiber: 1.7 g

Mocha Pie

If you love coffee with chocolate, you'll love this rich pie. Good quality, strong decaffeinated coffee is the key to success in the recipe. To chop the chocolate, use a cutting board and a sharp knife. I like to make the pie with the Pecan Crust on Page 112.

Makes 9 servings

1 Pecan Crust (Page 112)
2 packets unflavored gelatin
1/2 cup cold water
6 oz cream cheese
Scant 2/3 cup Splenda
2 cups strong, hot decaffeinated coffee
3/4 cup whipping cream
1/2 oz (1/2 square) semisweet baking chocolate, finely chopped

1. Make pecan crust, and set aside.
2. In a 1-cup measure or similar small bowl, soften gelatin in cold water. Reserve.
3. In a food processor, process cream cheese and Splenda until smooth. Reserve.
4. In a medium bowl, combine coffee and gelatin mixture, and stir until thoroughly dissolved, about 1 minute. Cool coffee mixture slightly in the refrigerator. With food processor running, slowly pour coffee mixture into cream cheese mixture, processing until well combined.
5. In a mixer bowl, beat whipping cream until stiff. Beat in coffee mixture. Pour into prepared pie shell or directly into pie plate. Sprinkle chocolate over pie top. Chill until firm, about 2 or 3 hours.

Carbs: 7.8 g   Protein: 3.8 g   Calories: 309.4   Fiber: 1.8 g

Cheesecake

The first low-carbohydrate dessert I thought of making was cheesecake. Here's my easy and very tasty version. The recipe calls for a pecan crust, which I use when I serve the cheesecake to company. If I'm just making it for a family dessert, I usually omit the crust. I mix the batter in a food processor because that allows me to take off the lemon zest in strips, coarsely chop it, then finish the chopping with the other ingredients in the batter. If you use a mixer instead, you must grate the lemon zest before adding it. After baking, the top of the cheesecake will be slightly cracked, but the cracks are covered by the sour cream layer.

Makes 10 servings

1/2 cup chopped pecans, ground in a food processor
24 oz cream cheese, softened (3 8-oz pks)
3/4 cup Splenda
Zest of 1 lemon (yellow part only) chopped
1 1/2 tsp vanilla extract
4 large eggs
1 1/2 cups commercial sour cream
2 Tbsp Splenda
Strawberries for garnish (optional)

1. Heat oven to 300 degrees. Butter bottom and sides of a 9 1/2-inch springform pan. Sprinkle bottom evenly with ground pecans, using fingers to distribute them evenly.
2. In a food processor bowl, process cream cheese, Splenda, lemon peel, and vanilla until fluffy, stopping to scrape down the sides of the bowl as necessary. Beat in eggs, 1 at a time, scraping down the sides of the bowl as needed, until well combined.
3. Carefully pour mixture over pecans. Bake about 1 hour or until a toothpick inserted in the center comes out clean. Cool to room temperature for 20 minutes.
4. Meanwhile, heat oven to 350 degrees. In a small bowl,

combine sour cream and Splenda. Spread sour cream mixture evenly over cheesecake. Bake 5 minutes until sour cream is slightly set. Cool at room temperature 20 minutes. Refrigerate at least 3 hours before serving. If you need to cool the cheesecake more quickly, you can put it in the freezer for half an hour after cooling at room temperature. Then remove from the freezer, cover, and refrigerate. Cheesecake will keep in the refrigerator for 3 or 4 days.

Carbs: 6.5 g   Protein: 9.1 g   Calories: 377.3   Fiber: 0.7 g

Lemon Mousse

There are certain flavors we all remember fondly from our childhoods. This dessert tastes a lot like one my mom used to make. Since it requires whipping 2 different mixtures, I make it using a mixer and a food processor. When I want to make Lemon Mousse, and I'm in a hurry, I use a 2-quart casserole dish instead of a mold, let it set, and spoon it out to serve.

Makes 9 or 10 servings

1 packet unflavored gelatin
1 cup boiling water
1/4 cup lemon juice
3/4 cup whipping cream
1 8-oz pkg cream cheese, at room temperature, cut into about
    4 chunks
1/2 cup Splenda
1 Tbsp vanilla extract
1 cup evaporated milk
Narrow strips of lemon zest, strawberries, or sliced kiwi for
    garnish (optional)

1. In a 2-cup measure or similar small bowl, combine gelatin
   and water. Stir until gelatin is completely melted, about 1
   minute. Stir in lemon juice. Refrigerate to chill slightly.
   Check gelatin occasionally. If it begins to set, remove it
   from the refrigerator.
2. In a mixer bowl, beat whipping cream until stiff. Reserve.
3. In a food processor bowl, whip together cream cheese,
   Splenda, and vanilla. With processor running, gradually add
   evaporated milk through feed tube, stopping and scraping
   down the sides of the bowl as necessary. With processor
   running, gradually add gelatin mixture, stopping and
   scraping down sides of bowl if necessary.
4. Add cream cheese mixture to whipped cream, and beat

119

together with mixer until well combined.
5. Pour into a 7-cup mold, and chill until set, about 2 or 3 hours.
6. To unmold, set mold in a bowl of warm water, then shake to determine when contents loosen. Invert on a serving plate. Garnish with lemon zest, a few strawberries, or kiwi slices if desired.

Carbs: 7.1 g   Protein: 4.3 g   Calories: 208.4   Fiber: 0 g

Strawberry Mousse

Here's a wonderfully rich and delicately flavored molded dessert. If you don't want to go to the trouble of unmolding it, you can make it in a large casserole and spoon out portions. One nice thing about this dessert and many of the others in this chapter is that you can make them a day ahead and stash them in the refrigerator until needed.

Makes 9 servings

1 packet unflavored gelatin
1 cup boiling water
2 Tbsp lemon juice
1 cup whipping cream
1 8-oz package cream cheese, at room temperature, cut into about 4 chunks
1/2 cup Splenda
1 1/2 tsp vanilla extract
1 1/2 cups sliced strawberries
Strawberry slices for garnish (optional)

1. In a 2-cup measure or similar small bowl, combine gelatin and water. Stir until gelatin is completely melted, about 1 minute. Stir in lemon juice. Refrigerate to chill slightly. Check gelatin occasionally. If it begins to set, remove it from the refrigerator.
2. In a mixer bowl, beat whipping cream until stiff. Reserve.
3. In a food processor bowl, whip together cream cheese, Splenda, and vanilla, stopping and scraping down the sides of the bowl as necessary. Gradually add gelatin mixture through feed tub. Add strawberries and process until pureed. Add cream cheese mixture to whipped cream, and beat together with mixer until well combined.
4. Pour into a 7-cup mold. Chill until set, about 2 or 3 hours. To unmold, dip the mold briefly in warm water. Run a knife around the edge of the mold to loosen. Turn upside

down on a serving plate, and shake if necessary to unmold. Garnish with strawberry slices if desired.

Carbs: 5.7 g   Protein: 2.7 g   Calories: 197.8   Fiber: 0.6 g

Ice Cream

The ice creams in this book were designed using a Cuisinart and a Krups ice cream maker. These machines are easy and convenient to use because there's no fussing with ice and salt. You simply freeze the ice cream container ahead of time. When you're ready to make ice cream, just remove the container from the freezer, and fill with the desired mixture. Follow directions for freezing time that come with your machine. I find the Cuisinart machine freezes ice cream in about 20 minutes. The Krups takes less time.

Below are 3 rich and creamy ice cream mixtures, all of which are sweetened with Splenda. The Splenda produces great tasting ice cream, but it does tend to stick to the sides of the container as it freezes. Use a rigid plastic spatula to get the ice cream out of the container as quickly as possible after it freezes. After the ice cream has been in the freezer for several hours, it will freeze very hard and must be microwaved briefly in order to scoop it from the container. For this reason, I freeze each batch in 2 small containers rather than one larger one, because the lesser volume of ice cream is softened more quickly in the microwave (about 20 to 30 seconds).

You can serve ice cream plain or with DaVinci sugar free syrups and chopped nuts.

Since directions for all 3 ice creams are the same, they appear only following the recipe for coffee ice cream.

All ice cream recipes make 4 or 5 servings

Vanilla Ice Cream

2 cups heavy cream
1 cup half and half
3/4 cup Splenda
2 tsp vanilla extract

Carbs: 11.1 g   Protein: 4.2 g   Calories: 513   Fiber: 0 g

Strawberry Ice Cream

I've called for 1 cup of Splenda in this ice cream. With very sweet spring strawberries, you may want to start with 3/4 cup, then add more if necessary.

2 cups heavy cream
1 cup half and half
1 cup Splenda
2 cups sliced fresh strawberries, chopped in food processor
1 tsp vanilla extract

Carbs: 14 g   Protein: 3.7 g   Calories: 430   Fiber: 1.4 g

Coffee Ice Cream

2 cups heavy cream
1 cup half and half
3/4 cup Splenda
1 Tbsp plus 1 tsp instant decaf coffee crystals
1 tsp vanilla extract

Carbs: 11.5 g   Protein: 4.4 g   Calories: 513.8   Fiber: 0 g

1. In an 8-cup measure or large bowl, stir together all ice cream ingredients. Turn on the motor and pour the mixture into the ice cream container. Process according to machine directions, or until desired consistency is reached. Quickly remove ice cream from container. Eat at once, or freeze until firm. Ice cream will keep in the freezer for up to 2 weeks.

Frozen Strawberry Cream Pie

With the advent of pasteurized eggs, it's once again safe to include raw egg whites in recipes. Here I've used them in frozen strawberry pie. One thing I've discovered is that pasteurized eggs are more slippery than regular eggs, so handle them carefully while separating them. Also, be sure to beat the egg whites until stiff peaks form. Be patient, as this takes time. If you don't have an ice cream maker, and you're craving ice cream, this pie makes a great substitute. But it's also a wonderful dessert on its own.

Makes 8 or 9 servings

2 cups sliced fresh strawberries
2 pasteurized egg whites
1 Tbsp lemon juice
1 cup Splenda
1 1/2 cups whipping cream
2 tsp vanilla extract

1. In a food processor, process strawberries just until chopped. Set aside.
2. In an absolutely fat-free mixer bowl, beat egg whites until frothy. Add lemon juice. Gradually add Splenda, continuing to beat until mixture forms stiff peaks.
3. In a separate bowl, whip cream and vanilla until stiff. Blend in strawberries by hand. With a rubber spatula, blend in egg white mixture. Pour mixture into a 9-inch pie plate, and smooth out surface with a spatula. Place in freezer for about 4 hours or until frozen. When partially frozen, cover with plastic wrap. To serve, thaw in the microwave at high power for 20 seconds. Or set on the counter for 10 minutes. Cut with a sharp knife.

Carbs: 7.5 g   Protein: 2 g   Calories: 184.7   Fiber: 0.9 g

Sweetened Whipped Cream

Here's a rich and easy topping for cake, pie, or fruit such as strawberries or raspberries.

Makes 6 to 12 servings

2 cups heavy whipping cream
2 Tbsp Splenda
2 tsp vanilla extract

1. In a mixer bowl, combine the whipping cream, Splenda, and vanilla. Whip on high speed until stiff peaks form. Cream will keep in a covered container in the refrigerator for 2 or 3 days.

Carbs: 3.2 g   Protein: 1.6 g   Calories: 280.2   Fiber: 0 g

Pecan Cake

You'd never know this spice and nut cake is made with no flour.

Makes 8 or 9 servings

1 1/2 cups ground pecans
1/2 tsp ground ginger
1/2 tsp ground cinnamon
1/8 tsp salt
9 large eggs, separated
1 cup Splenda
1 tsp vanilla extract

1. Preheat oven to 325 degrees. Generously butter the bottom and sides of a 9-inch springform pan. Set aside.
2. In a medium bowl, mix together nuts, ginger, cinnamon, and salt, and set aside.
3. In an absolutely fat free mixer bowl, beat egg whites until stiff. Set aside.
4. In another mixer bowl, beat egg yolks until light. Gradually add Splenda and vanilla, beating until light and creamy.
5. Beat in nut mixture until well mixed. Vigorously fold egg whites into batter using a rubber spatula, working until the egg whites are incorporated.
6. Turn batter into springform pan. Bake for 50 minutes. Cool on a wire rack. Run a knife along the edges of the pan to loosen the cake before removing.

Carbs: 7.1 g   Protein: 9.3 g   Calories: 240.2   Fiber: 2.3 g

Creme Anglaise

This classic custard is marvelous with sliced strawberries or simply on its own. It's also used in the Pecan Custard Tarts on Page 133. Although it's not absolutely necessary to strain the custard through a sieve, this makes the texture smoother.

Makes 7 servings, 1/4 cup each

4 large egg yolks
Generous 1/3 cup Splenda
3/4 cup half and half
3/4 cup heavy cream
1/4 tsp salt
1 1/2 tsp vanilla extract

1. Place egg yolks in a mixer bowl, and beat with an electric mixer 3 or 4 minutes.
2. In the top of a double boiler, combine Splenda, half and half, cream, and salt. Stir to mix well. Place over boiling water, making sure water in bottom of double boiler does not touch top pot.
3. Heat to a simmer, stirring with a wooden spoon. Remove top pot from boiling water. Stir 1/2 cup of hot mixture into egg yolks. Stir this mixture back into remaining hot mixture. Adjust heat to medium high, and cook about 3 minutes, stirring with a wooden spoon.
4. Remove from heat, and stir in vanilla. Pour through a sieve into a small bowl. Cover and refrigerate.

Carbs: 3.4 g   Protein: 2.9 g   Calories: 162.8   Fiber: 0 g

Tart Shells

Phyllo dough is so thin that it's very low in carbs. Here I've used it to make elegant and easy tart shells that I'm sure will make their way into the lo-carb pantheon. If you don't leave enough time (5 hours) to thaw the phyllo dough at room temperature, you can speed the process in the microwave on the defrost setting. I use the shells to make the Strawberry Tarts on Page 131 and the Pecan Cream Cheese Tarts on Page 134.

Makes 12 servings

3 large phyllo sheets, thawed
1/4 cup melted butter

1. Butter a 12-cup standard muffin tin. Set aside. Preheat the oven to 400 degrees.
2. Lay the phyllo on a large plastic cutting board or other flat surface. Using a sharp scissors or a sharp knife, cut each pastry sheet into 4- to 4 1/2-inch squares. A narrow edge will remain on each sheet. Discard this extra dough. Stack the squares, and keep them covered with wax paper and a damp tea towel until you are ready for them. With a pastry brush, brush 3 squares with butter. Place the squares on top of each other, rotating them slightly so that the corners are facing in different directions. Gently press the squares into a muffin cup, making a basket. Repeat the process to make 12 cups.
3. Bake on the center oven rack for 4 or 5 minutes or until the edges of the cups begin to crisp. Cool slightly and carefully remove tart shells from muffin cups. Shells can be cooled slightly and filled about 20 minutes before serving. Or they can be cooled, removed from the muffin tins, covered with plastic wrap, and stored in the refrigerator for 3 or 4 days before using.

Carbs: 2.3 g   Protein: 0.4 g   Calories: 48.9   Fiber: 0.1 g

Strawberry Tarts

These strawberry tarts make a festive finale to a company meal. Do not fill the tart shells until just before serving as the Creme Anglaise will soften the shells.

Makes 12 servings

1 recipe Tart Shells (Page 130)
1 recipe Creme Anglaise (Page 129)
1 1/2 to 2 cups strawberries

1. Make Tart Shells. Reserve.
2. Make Creme Anglaise. Reserve
3. Just before serving, fill each shell with 3 tablespoons Creme Anglaise. Top with 2 tablespoons (or more, if desired) sliced strawberries.

Carbs: 5.6 g   Protein: 2.1 g   Calories: 149.5   Fiber: 0.5 g

Strawberry Whipped Cream Tarts

Here's an even easier strawberry tart. Do not fill the tart shells until just before serving as the custard will soften the shells.

1 Recipe Tart Shells (Page 130)
1 recipe Sweetened Whipped Cream (Page 127)
1 1/2 to 2 cups strawberries

1. Make Tart Shells. Reserve.
2. Make Sweetened Whipped Cream. Reserve.
3. Just before serving, fill each shell with 3 tablespoons Sweetened Whipped Cream. Top with 2 tablespoons (or more, if desired) sliced strawberries.

Carbs: 5.2 g   Protein: 1.3 g   Calories: 194.6   Fiber: 0.5 g

Pecan Custard Tarts

Here's another rich dessert featuring the Tart Shells on Page 130. Do not assemble the tarts until just before serving, as the Creme Anglaise will soften the shells.

Makes 12 servings

1 recipe Toffee-Flavored Pecans (Page 111)
1 recipe Tart Shells (Page 130)
1 recipe Creme Anglaise (Page 129)

1. Make Toffee-Flavored Pecans. Coarsely chop pecans. Reserve.
2. Make Tart Shells. Reserve.
3. Make Creme Anglaise
4. Just before serving, fill each shell with 3 tablespoons custard. Sprinkle chopped pecans evenly over custard.

Carbs: 5.6 g   Protein: 3 g   Calories: 225.2   Fiber: 1.1 g

Pecan Cream Cheese Tarts

These rich tarts have a pleasing combination of tastes and textures.
They're made with my Toffee-Flavored Pecans and Tart Shells.

Makes 12 servings

1 recipe Toffee-Flavored Pecans (Page 111)
1 recipe Tart Shells (Page 130)
12 oz cream cheese, at room temperature
1/2 cup heavy cream
1/4 cup Splenda

1. Make Toffee-Flavored Pecans. Coarsely chop pecans.
   Reserve.
2. Make Tart Shells. Reserve.
3. In a medium bowl, combine cream cheese, cream, and
   Splenda. With a fork stir together until well blended.
4. At this point, all ingredients can be refrigerated separately.
   Or tart shells can be filled up to 4 or 5 hours in advance.
   To fill shells, divide cream cheese mixture evenly among
   tart cups. Sprinkle chopped pecans evenly over cream
   cheese mixture. Just before serving, heat the tarts in their
   muffin cups or on a baking sheet for 5 or 6 minutes in a
   350-degree oven. Serve warm.

Carbs: 5.2 g   Protein: 3.7 g   Calories: 265.2   Fiber: 1.1 g

Hot Mocha

A nice substitute for hot chocolate. Since the cocoa tends to settle to the bottom of the mug, you may want to stir from time to time.

Makes 1 serving

1 cup hot decaf coffee
1 tsp cocoa powder (not drink mix)
2 Tbsp heavy cream
Splenda to taste

1. In a mug, stir cocoa into coffee until dissolved. Stir in cream and Splenda.

Carbs: 2.2 g   Protein: 1 g   Calories: 109.9   Fiber: 0 g

HELPFUL LO-CARB PRODUCTS

To keep up-to-date on these and other products, check with the Lo-Carb Cook website:

http://www.locarbcook.com

DaVinci Gourmet Sugar-Free Flavored Syrups

These syrups are wonderful for making snow cones, Italian sodas (soda water, flavored syrup, and cream), and as a topping for ice cream. DaVinci Gourmet makes a wide variety of flavors--from Caramel and Butter Rum to Peach, Strawberry, Raspberry, and Chocolate.

More information: 800-640-6779; http://www.davincigourmet.com

La Tortilla Factory

The whole wheat, high fiber tortillas made by this factory are fantastically low in carbs.

More information: 800-446-1516; http://www.latortillafactory.com/

Nellie and Joe's Famous Key West Lime Juice

If you love the taste of key lime pie, you'll want to keep this wonderful, tart juice on hand. According to the label, the juice has no carbs.

More information: 800-Lime-Pie; http://www.keylimejuice.com

Newsoms Peanuts

This company makes wonderful southern-style peanuts that are perfect for munching. Alas, they have no web site.

More information: 757-654-6564